4/03

D1442643

COMPLETE GUIDE TO FISHING

Flyfishing

COMPLETE GUIDE TO FISHING

Flyfishing

MASON CREST PUBLISHERS, INC.

COMPLETE GUIDE TO FISHING – **Flyfishing** has been originated, produced and designed by AB Nordbok, Gothenburg, Sweden.

Publisher
Gunnar Stenmar

Editorial chief
Anders Walberg

Design, setting & photowork:
Reproman AB, Gothenburg, Sweden

Translator:
Jon van Leuven

Nordbok would like to express sincere thanks to all persons and companies who have contributed in different ways to the production of this book.

World copyright © 2002
Nordbok International,
P.O.Box 7095,
SE-402 32 Gothenburg, Sweden.

Published in the United States by
Mason Crest Publishers, Inc.
370 Reed Road, Broomall, PA 19008
(866) MCP-BOOK (toll free)
www.masoncrest.com

First printing
1 2 3 4 5 6 7 8 9 10
Library of Congress Cataloging-in-Publication Data on file at
the Library of Congress

ISBN 1-59084-495-5

Printed and bound in Jordan 2002

Contents

Preface

Watching a practitioner of flyfishing present his or her flies to the fish with billowing, harmonic movements is a fascinating and beautiful sight.

For the confirmed flyfisherman, the great adventure beckons from almost every body of water. Each movement of the water becomes an attraction; any glimpse of a shadow on the bottom is a challenge. With endless rapture we can devote days and weeks, even months and years, to attempts at catching fish with our cleverly created flies.

And flyfishing is certainly more a way of living than just a hobby or sport. Being a flyfisherman involves a very special attitude toward nature's ever equally lovely, intriguing and unpredictable diversity.

Today there is no kind of fishing that has as many common features and as few national characteristics as flyfishing. The prey of this art is largely the same around the world, like the equipment and the types of water in which we usually choose to wet our flies.

The evolution of modern flyfishing

Progress in improving fishing equipment was quite slow. In the mid-1660s, however, hooks began to be made more durable by hardening them. Plagues and fires forced needlemakers, among others, to move out of London. Redditch soon became a center of hook-making, and the old handicraft of smithing was transformed into a large scale operation. Industrialization also brought with it improvements in the quality of hooks: they became thinner and lighter, though still thick and unwieldy compared with those of today.

Even if both Berner and Walton/Cotton showed great interest in the insects taken by fish, it was first in 1747 that the initial book on flytying first appeared, The *Art of Angling* by Richard Bowlker. This is widely regarded as the first handbook on the subject and something of a trendmaker. He not only presented a list of his own flies, indicating some knowledge of entomology, but gave direct instructions for special types of fishing, such as upstream fishing.

The rods which were used during the eighteenth century were primarily for the purpose of taking up the fish's strike. On the whole, flyfishing in those days bore little resemblance to that of today. The line and fly were not cast, but swung out to the presumed holding spot of the fish. Only at the end of the century did small primitive reels began to be manufactured, with room for storing a small amount of line. At about the same time, it had been discovered that the lines could be tapered by twining in more horsehairs at the middle than at the end.

By the outset of the nineteenth century, the rod's length had been considerably shortened from 16-18 to 11-12 feet (around 5 to 3.5 metres). There were frequent experiments with different kinds of rod materials such as greenheart, hickory and bamboo. In the mid-1840s, an American violinmaker managed to construct the first split-cane rod by gluing bamboo ribs together. This was a real breakthrough, as a perfect rod material had now been found along with a superior method of construction in order to build really strong, practical rods.

Greenwell's Glory, one of the classic English wet flies which are still popular among many lfyfishermen.

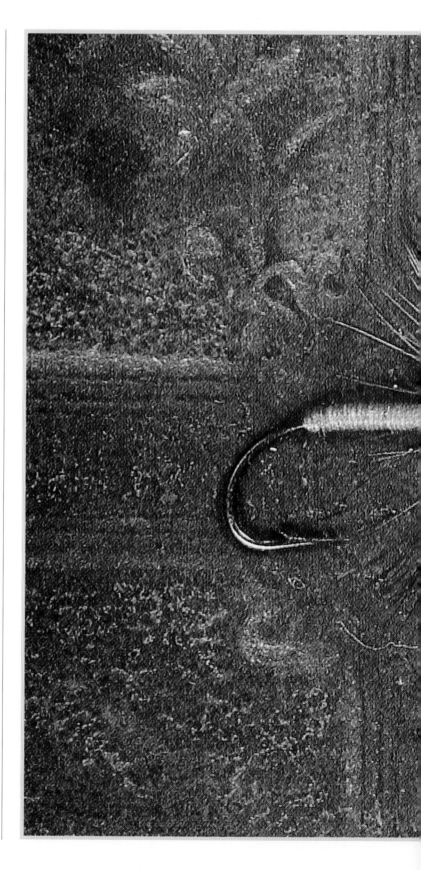

Split-cane rods, compared with earlier types, were light and pliable. In addition, they cast significantly better than their predecessors. However, they were still heavy and hard to handle as casting tools. Despite their overall advantage, it was to be some years before their production could be effectivized to make mass manufacture profitable. Two not entirely unknown names figure in this connection: the Americans Charles Orvis and Hiram Leonard. After about another decade, an Englishman named Hardy began his production of quality rods in the British Isles.

It was not only the development of the fly rod which started things moving in the mid-nineteenth century. Lines were also greatly improved. Thanks to the introduction of oiled silk lines, the casting length could be as much as tripled. More or less simultaneously, the horsehair was replaced by silk gut. Today's modern flyfishing had thus begun to take shape.

Flyfishing as a whole underwent extensive changes during the nineteenth century. The development of equipment, the interest in entomology, the creation of new fly patterns and techniques are all indications of this. A further factor, to be sure, was that flyfishing began to be popular in the true sense of the word. But with the popularization of flyfishing, the distance widened between it and other kinds of sportfishing. It became snobbish, ceremonial, and regarded as a fine art. There were echoes from the days of Berner: such a noble sport should be conducted and perfected by gentlemen.

Flyfishing tended ever more to become a science. Alfred Ronald was the first author to point out the relevance of insect breeding. His book of 1836 was, in fact, the first entomological description of insects in nature and their imaginary equivalents. Ronald's book inevitably increased the interest in insect studies. It suddenly became a matter of great concern to tie exact insect imitations by carefully observing all sorts of flying creatures at the water and recreating these faithfully for the fish.

During the second half of the nineteenth century, a lively debate blossomed about how the fly should be laid out. Upstream casting, downstream casting, and casting more or less across the stream were important questions. It was W. C. Stewart who made himself the champion of the upstream cast in his book *Practical Arglirg* (1857) which presented the technique and its advantages: by approaching the fish from the rear it is easier to imitate the insects' natural route downstream, and playing can occur without disturbing the fish upstre-

Izaak Walton was no devoted flyfisherman, but he undoubtedly became one of the great founding fathers of sportfishing. In the inset picture below, we see his fishing basket, now kept at the Flyfisher's Club in London.

am (that is, in as yet unfished water). Stewart was also of the opinion that it was more important to show the insect's size, form and appearance than to tie exact imitations.

The reign of the dry fly

Around 1860, dry-fly fishing began to take off in southern England. This new technique gathered ever more enthusiasts, and it did not take many decades before dry flies became ubiquitous, not least in English chalk streams. In the wake of this innovation, there followed a total devaluation of all that wet flies and wet-fly fishing stood for. It was regarded as unsporting and virtually immoral to fish with any kind of wet fly.

It had long been noticed that fish gladly took a wet fly just when it had landed on the water surface or had broken through. The new technique started by trying to get wet flies to fish dry. The fly was dried by means of a number of air casts, then landed on the water and floated until it eventually got soaked and sank under its own weight. Although dry-fly fishing is generally thought to have been "discovered" in England during the mid-nineteenth century, there is proof that the technique was used in Spain already during the seventeenth century, according to the *El Manuscrito de Astorga* (1624).

In any case, the basis of today's dry-fly fishing was developed in the south English chalk streams, for example at Itchen where there were plenty of hungry - although sometimes quite selective - trout and loads of insects. As the fish "learned" to see the difference between real and imitation prey, the wet flies which were dried out by air casting fished less well. The "true and proper" dry fly therefore came as a fresh start, not only because it was a new fashion in itself, but because it fished more effectively.

As to who was actually the first to introduce the dry fly is, as with so much else, a controversial question. Some maintain that it was Pullman in his *Vade Mecum of Fly Fishing for Trout* (1851), while others claim that it was a professional fly tier, James Ogden, who made the innovation. At all events, it was an article in *The Field* during 1857 written by Francis Francis which spread the principles of dry-fly fishing beyond a rather small circle of fishermen.

What then of Frederic M. Halford, widely considered the indisputable father of dry-fly fishing? The fact is that he, according to reliable sources, did not attempt dry-fly fishing until 1868 - that is, several years after the "discovery" of dry

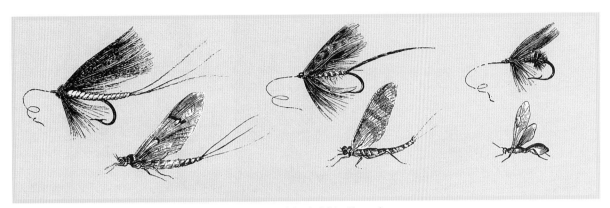

Early attempts were made to tie flies that imitated the natural food of fish. Shown here are some flies from the late seventeenth century, together with their real prototypes.

flies. Yet what Halford did do was to perfect the technique with floating dun hooks.

The last decades of the nineteenth century brought a strong upsurge in flyfishing, not least due to Halford and the group of outwardly passionate flyfishermen who surrounded him. Enormous pains were taken to develop both equipment and techniques. The oiled silk lines were improved, body materials were tested which did not draw in water, and new techniques were sought for tying more durable flies. Halford became a dry-fly fisherman by profession. At the age of 45 he retired in order to devote all his time to the sport. This unbelievable commitment, of course, yielded returns. Together with his fishing friends he developed a standard in regard to rods, lines and flies which maintained its relevance long into our century.

His passionate activity also resulted in a couple of books which are regarded today as established works for flyfishermen. His first and best known, *Floating Flies* and *How to Dress Them* (1886), presented, after years of intensive insect studies in the chalk stream district of Hampshire, nearly 100 duns and spinners. Three years later came his *Dry Fly Fishing in Theory and Practice* (1889): here Halford described in a systematic way all the phases of dry-fly fishing. This is a virtually comprehensive work on fishing with dry flies in the English chalk streams. On certain waters, such as slowflowing streams with selective trout, it is still of great value.

We can say without exaggeration that Halford released an avalanche: interest in dry-fly fishing grew at a raging pace. It became modern to collect insects and make naturally faithful copies with Halford's theories of imitation and his flytying technique as a basis. However, the other side of the coin beca-

me a fanatical attitude that only dry-fly fishing was the correct way to seek contact with the fish. True believers would never have picked up a wet fly with a pair of pincers.

For this tragic development, Halford bears great responsibility, since in his later days he became quite intolerant of divergent opinions. The "father of dry-fly fishing" was unimpressed by wet flies and nymphs. Rather he tried to combat them as if they were a dangerous nuisance in the fly box. Fishing with dry flies for standing fish was the only proper method for him, while downstream fishing with a wet fly was not only ineffective but also a destructive and immoral form of flyfishing.

The challenging nymph

Along with the strong expansion and popularization of flyfishing, equipment was improved as well. Rods became easier to handle and the lines smoother to cast. Not least the Americans contributed much to these developments. When this fishing tackle came to England around 1900, nymph fishing slowly began to arise.

A central figure in nymph fishing was George Edward Mackenzie Skues, the technique's inventor and chief theoretician. Born in 1858, he died in 1949 a full 91 years old and it may be surmised that his success at fishing was one reason for his long life.

Like dry-fly fishing, nymph fishing was developed in the English chalk streams. This is because such streams are fine to experiment in, with their clear water, abundant insect life, and selective fish which have become familiar with hooks due to the active flyfishing.

In the late 1800s, Skues began to experiment. He asked

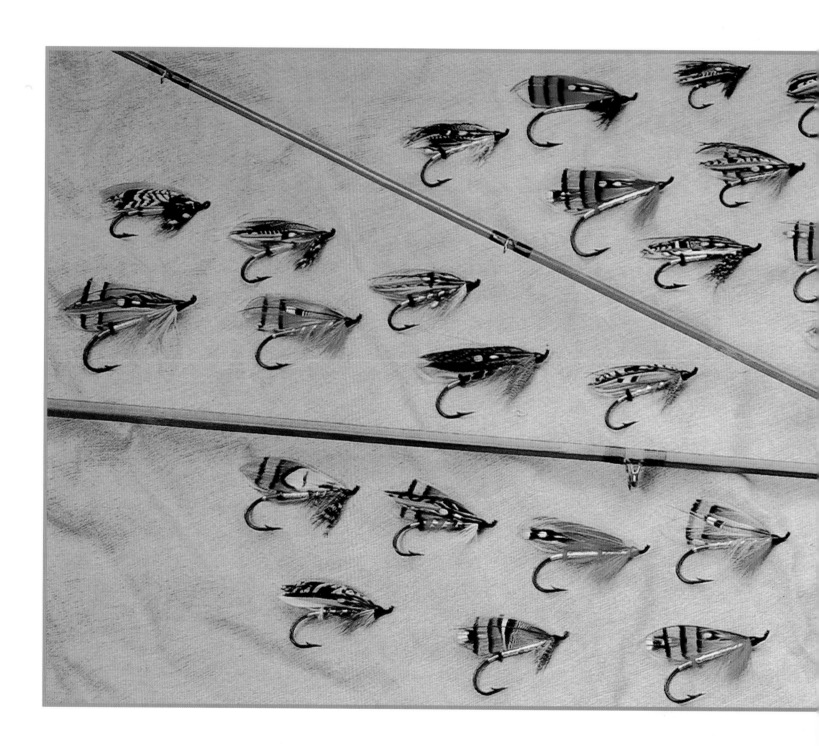

Fully dressed classic salmon flies.

himself: why fish with dry flies when the quarry take food in or just under the water surface?

The idea of fishing with a wet fly when the quarry did not take insects on the water surface was, at the time, heretical to many flybishermen in conservative England. But this did not prevent Skues from pursuing his research: he developed methods and patterns on the theory that fish were occasionally more interested in the hathing insects than in the already hatched ones. Thus soft-hackled, unweighted flies became the alternative to dry flies.

Flyfishing in the United States

The English colonists who reached the North American continent during the eighteenth and nineteenth centuries naturally brought with them a knowledge of, and interest in, flyfishing to their new land. The sport had taken root by the end of the eighteenth century, and it is even thought that special shops then existed for flyfishing materials and equipment.

Serious fishing with a fly began in the United States around 1850. At this time the Wild West was still living up to its name. It was therefore mainly in the eastern parts of the country that people diverted themselves by fishing with

rod, line and hook. In the more civilized Eastern states, people also began to realize that flyfishing was an unusually rewarding form of sportfishing.

In 1887 the book *Fly-Fishing and Fly-Making* by John H. Keene came out. Its main interest is that it shows that people in the USA had come farther in the development of flyfishing than we have tended to believe. The book not only describes how to tie dry flies, for example, but also displays a degree of innovative thinking which was long thought to have been reserved for greater luminaries such as Theodore Gordon.

Despite the country's late entry into flyfishing history in relation to England, the refinement of rods, spools, reels and lines was steadily driven forth. As mentioned previously, it was an American violin maker who, in the mid-1840s, made the first split-cane rods. After about 25 years, they began to be mass-produced and the rods were improved in features like casting ability and weight - so much that the English began to

George M. Kelson.

import them around the turn of the century. English rods at the time were long, heavy and stiff; thus gradually the English took over the American type of rod, which many have seen as a prerequisite for the development of nymph fishing.

The American equivalent of the chalk streams in Hampshire became the Catskill rivers in the state of New York. Rivers such as the Neversink and the Beaverkill are today classic waters in the history of American flyfishing.

In Europe and England, the brown trout was the target for the hardily casting flyfisherman. This species, however, did not originally exist in the USA. There, people fished instead for brook trout in the eastern states, and for steelhead or cutthroat in the west.

With the growing popularity of fishing, the supply of brook trout in particular decreased drastically. During the 1880s, trout consequently began to be imported from Europe. The first fish were taken from Germany and the species is thus called the "German trout".

As brown trout, and later rainbow trout, were implanted in rivers, the waters became harder to fish. The traditional downstream wet-fly fishing proved ineffective. These trout were simply not as easy to fool as the brook trout, and flyfishermen were slowly but surely forced to reconsider.

One of those who perhaps came to mean most for the development of American flyfishing was Theodore Gordon. He was something of a loner who, in 1905, settled on the Neversink in order to be able to tie flies and do his fishing in peace and quiet. His literary production was primarily a number of articles in the journals *Forest and Stream* (USA) and *Fishing Gazette* (England). He also corresponded fluently with Halford and Skues. Through this lofty correspondence with two of the great men of flyfishing, he acquired a fine insight into the development of English flyfishing.

At the end of the nineteenth century, Gordon obtained some 50 dry flies from Halford. However, these were tied according to English conditions and were therefore poor imitations of the insects which existed in Gordon's home waters. As a fly tier, though, Gordon began to tie his own dry flies with Halford's technique, but modelled on local insects He created many original patterns, the best known being Gordon Quill, and he also developed the so-called "bumble puppies" in the Neversink. These flies were the predecessors of the bucktail patterns, subsequently so much used.

Gordon laid the foundations for the Catskill School, which came to have a huge impact on American flytying. The fanaticism which marked English dry-fly fishing never reached the USA and there were thus larger possibilities of experimenting. The results were significantly more sparingly dressed flies than the typical dry flies from the vHalford epoch in England.

Another American who has acquired a leading place in the history of flyfishing is George LaBranche. In 1914 his first book came out: *The Dry Fly and Fast Waters*. He is regarded for this and other reasons as the man who made American dry-fly fishing really popular. In the book was presented a technique for effective dry-fly fishing even in relatively rapid waterways. It differed in various respects from Halford's theories, which were primarily suited to the English chalk streams.

LaBranche's fishing technique was distinctive in many ways from the Catskill school, one essential difference being the size and bushy appearance of the flies, which made them float high and remain easily visible to the fish. LaBranche also belongs to those who developed the technique of fishing salmon with dry flies.

In general a different style of flyfishing and flytying arose in the USA as compared with England. An example is the special type of wet flies called bucktails and streamers. They grew up in America during the 1920s and are refinements of the classic wet fly. Observant flyfishermen had discovered that wet flies with silver or gold bodies could be identified as fry by the fish. Gradually there arose a whole lot of different patterns of bucktails (hairwing flies) and of streamers (featherwing flies) which, in one way or another, imitated fish fry in different species and stages.

In addition to those authors already named, Edward R. Hewitt had a great influence on this progress. He was a contemporary of LaBranche, and was one of the great flyfishing authors between the two World Wars. Today he is perhaps best known for his division of flyfishing development into three phases: (1) as many fish as possible, (2) as big fish as possible, (3) as difficult as possible to catch. Hewitt also advanced the view that the presentation of the fly was extremely important: the main thing according to him was not to have as great a range of flies as possible, but to have a smaller number and be able to present them correctly.

Flyfishing is a passion for many people - and for some, a real addiction - which often lasts a lifetime and can seldom be completely cured...

The flies –
our deceptive imitations

There are many thousands of fly patterns around the world. Every day new materials and patterns appear. The range is so wide and difficult to survey that a newcomer may well feel confused when he or she is choosing flies for the first time.

However, flies and fly patterns are often two different things. Fly patterns are what you use as a model for tying; flies are what you fish with. All too many flyfishermen and fly tiers overlook this distinction. They place excessive faith in the fly pattern itself, and think more seldom about how the finished fly works and whether it is suitable for fishing.

Among us fly tiers are plenty of "pattern fanatics": fly tiers for whom a fly is acceptable only if tied exactly according to the rulebook, and then only with the correct materials. Thus they become slaves to the pattern, and are unable to tie a particular type of fly if they lack any of the often exotic materials which are prescribed.

It ought not to be that way - at least from the viewpoint of a flyfisherman. The fish are indifferent to tiny details and conceits; they are far more interested in the actual presentation of the fly than in the pattern. What counts for a fish is the total impression, not the absence of a few fibers or a peculiar feather.

Imitations or fantasy flies

If you tie flies for the sake of flytying, you obviously have to stick to the correct patterns and materials. Then it becomes a hobby in itself. But fishing has for many years suffered from the fact that authors are often more inclined to flytying than to fishing. The available literature has therefore given, at least to beginners at flyfishing and flytying, the mistaken impression that fly patterns are something sacred and inviolate.

Fortunately a clear change in this situation has taken place during recent years. New materials and tying methods have arrived, banishing the old classics into oblivion. These materials are easier to work with than the original ones, and are much more durable too.

Plastic tinsel does not break down like the old metal materials, even in the saltiest water. Stainless steel has shown the same advantage in regard to hooks. Polypropylene has revolutionized dry flies, for example, where it is lighter than water

and, moreover, is water-repellent. On the whole, synthetic materials have made life a lot happier for both the fly tier and flyfisherman.

In spite of that, many classics are still in our fly-boxes. They are flies which have been around for longer than most of us can remember flies so simple and ingenious that they still fish as well as on the day when they were first conceived. Often it is not a question of the actual pattern. These eternally young classics are types which be varied according to the conditions and can therefore cover a range of fishing situations. Just think of the "muddler", which can be tied in all conceivable circumstances - from the smallest to the largest - and is fished

A fly pattern can be created from various points of view. It may be a pure fantasy fly, or an exact imitation.

a situation where he or she was forced to get along with the materials at hand. Perhaps quite different materials would have been used if available at the time, and perhaps the finished fly would have been even better. So the fly tier ought to have a relaxed attitude towards the pattern. Flies are primarily intended to be used for fishing and, if one does not happen to have the prescribed material, one replaces it with something similar - maybe even better than the original material - for one's own fishing water!

A fly pattern can be created from various points of view. It may be a pure fantasy fly, or an exact imitation. The fly can be imagined to imitate the fish's natural prey, or it can be designed as a provocation. Thousands of fantasy flies have been conceived through the years, but very few have stood the test of time. England's bright red Cardinal, for example, has survived precisely because of its beautiful appearance and classic name. The same is true of a fly such as Silver Doctor, which is equally popular for brown trout, sea trout and salmon. It is obvious that the pretty colours are what have kept these flies in the fly-box, even more than their ability to catch fish, which is no better or worse than that of many other flies.

Things are different with the imitation flies, many of which have lasted remarkably well. This is especially true of dry flies and nymphs from the age of Halford and Skues. Although first tied around the turn of the century, they have nevertheless managed to retain their status for decades. It was, in fact, first when Swisher and Rickards created the famous "no hackle" dry flies that Halford's original dry flies became obsolete. Among other innovations, that of synthetic polypropylene - then called "phentex" - set the development in motion. Until then, natural materials had enjoyed a monopoly.

Good and bad imitations

On the whole, the classic English dry flies are incredibly poor imitations of real mayflies. Their dense hackle, which was needed to let them float at all, was enough to make them bad imitations. That they still could, and can, defeat shy and selective trout in the southern English chalk streams may tell us more about the fish than about the flies.

We usually say that dry flies float, but they very seldom do so. In order to float, a fly must be lighter than water, and this

both wet and dry. It is a good instance of a true classic: a fly type rather than a fly pattern.

Consequently, a fly pattern should be regarded mainly as a proposal, rather than as a prescription. It ought to be a starting point for individual interpretations. A pattern which has been thought out or developed in order to suit the discerning trout in a quiet English chalk stream cannot necessarily be transferred to other parts of the world. It must be adapted to the fish's size and the water's current speed, depth and clarity, to mention only a few local factors.

Lastly we should consider the way in which a particular fly pattern came into being. Often the fly's inventor has been in is far from true of ordinary dry flies. A conventionally hackled dry fly is heavier than water and cannot float. It does not sink simply because it is held up by the surface tension. It actually stands on the surface with its many hackle fibers, just as the real insect does with its legs. Both rest on an unbroken water surface and are so shaped that the surface tension supports them. As soon as the surface tension is broken, the fly or insect sinks.

The surface tension of water, however, varies a lot from place to place. The cleaner the water is, the stronger its surface tension, and therefore the greater its ability to support insects and dry flies. When the water is polluted in any way, the surface tension immediately decreases. Then dry flies have difficulty in staying afloat. But what is worse, the same applies to the real insects. Many of them become unable to complete their life cycle, since they are "caught" hanging in the water surface and remain hanging there while they hatch.

Flytiers should take account of this phenomenon. It means that dry flies must be hackled more densely for polluted than for clean water. Actually we may get along well enough without hackle, as the above-mentioned "no hackles" indicate. As their name implies, these flies have no hackle at all, but consist of a tail, a body, and a pair of conspicuous wings. They can still be made to rest superbly on the surface tension, although in an impregnated condition. At the same time, they are silhouetted to the fish, and this is far better than the hackle fibers' imitation of characteristic mayflies. Especially typical of these insects are their upright wings.

Sparsely tied flies are, as a rule, best for selective fish in clear, calm water. They imitate their natural prototypes better than do densely hackled flies, which merely give the fish a confused picture of something that might be edible. Even so, in many situations we are forced to depend on the latter kind of flies - for example in fast waters, where flies with little or no hackle sink instantly.

For such fishing, therefore, special dry flies have been developed, which can stay afloat even in a whirling current. Instances are Wulffs, Kolzer Fireflies, Goofus Bugs and various Irresistibles. These flies are all equipped with strong wings and tail, as well as dense and bushy hackle of the highest quality. This structure enables them to stand high on the water, and keeps them visible to both the fish and fisherman. In the case of Goofus Bugs and Irresistibles, a further step has been taken: they are provided with a sort of "life jacket", an air-fil-

Many flyfishermen think that conventionally hackled dry flies float - in other words, that they are lighter than water. But the truth is that they rest on water's surface tension.

led body of deer hair, which gives them volume and floating force when it really counts.

These ample "floaters" seldom resemble anything in particular, but rather resemble a morsel which the fish are reluctant to pass up. In fast waters, it is nevertheless unnecessary to use the exact imitations which are required in clear, calm water. Fish in a rapid current do not have time to study the fly - they must react fast, or else it is gone again!

But densely hackled flies can also be needed in still waters, for example when fishing with imitations of caddis flies. This often involves large insects that cause commotion when they flutter about, especially during egg laying. Such behavior can be imitated by allowing a dry fly to drag on the surface, a technique which calls for densely hackled flies that do not sink immediately.

Today it has become ever more common to tie certain types of flies with foam rubber such as "polycelon". In this way the finished fly is made to literally float, in contrast to normal dry flies which simply rest on the surface tension. Such an ability is used for flies that have to float on the surface - typical hatching nymphs, or heavy land insects like beetles and grasshoppers. The latter can often be served up to notable advantage with a clear, loud splash that draws the fish's attention to the fly. And this is a technique that demands self-buoyant flies: those with a body of cork or foam rubber, which is easier to work with and also lasts longer. Here is still another proof that synthetic materials have revolutionized flytying and given us completely new opportunities.

Color can trigger strikes

But what is it about our flies that gets fish to strike? An ethologist can provide some insight into this fascinating subject. Ethology is the science of animal behavior, and conducts research on why animals act as they do.

In one of the most classic ethological experiments, it was investigated how the stickleback reacts to different stimuli. As is well known, the male becomes extremely aggressive during the spawning period. He defends his territory and nest against all intruders, especially competing males.

*Dry flies can be tied in numerous ways. Here we see a traditional example (upper left),
a "no hackle" dry fly (lower left), and (at right) the two steps needed to tie a parachute-hackled dry fly.*

During spawning, the males are colored bright red on their bellies, while the females have a large, distended stomach full of eggs. It was studied how the sticklebacks reacted to various decoys. Some of these were exact imitations of males and females, whereas others bore little or no resemblance to them.

The experiment yielded interesting insights into the fish's ways of reacting. Not unexpectedly, close-imitation decoys with bright red colors triggered a violent reaction in the males, which naturally thought that the decoys were competing males. Moreover, decoys with a distended belly attracted great interest as if they were real females.

Yet the truly fascinating result was that perfect imitations did not release stronger reactions than did the less close imitations. It was the color which proved decisive for the males, and the shape for the females. Color and shape were the so-called "key stimuli" which triggered reactions the factors that determined whether there would be any reaction at all. As long as the decoy was red, and preferably bright red, the males showed violent reactions, ignoring all else.

One might think that sticklebacks are more primitive than the salmonoids which we try to catch with flies, but such is not the case. From a purely evolutionary standpoint, salmonoids are more primitive, and the stickleback is among the most advanced fish. The experimental results with sticklebacks can thus very well be applied to salmon and trout.

What can we learn from this as fly tiers and flyfishermen? Quite a lot. It is natural to attempt to imitate, as closely and detailed as possible, the animals which constitute fish food. The more a fly resembles its prototype, the better it fishes - for fish are not stupid, are they?

Well, fish are indeed stupid, at any rate by human standards. They cannot think in the sense of adding two and two. They learn from experience, but do not reason. They have no perspective on their situation and, instead of thinking, react

Opposite: To choose or not to choose the fly is the question.

Streamers may be very effective when the fishing is slow. They are easily visible and are frequently good imitations of small fish. Mickey Finn is undoubtedly a classic streamer that can lure fish to strike even when the water is relatively warm.

MICKEY FINN
Hook: streamer hook No. 6-12
Body: silver tinsel
Wing: three sections – yellow, red, and yellow –
of hair from polar bear, calf tail, or goat

to external influences. Whether we like it or not, a fish is a primitive machine, controlled by its environment. The frequent difficulty of catching it is due to various factors which we are seldom able to govern.

This logic serves simply to bring down to reality the controversial "imitation principle". Certainly it may be interesting to tie very exact imitations, but unfortunately the fish rarely set much store by them. From the experiment with sticklebacks, we saw that the color is the decisive key stimulus. If we look at our own flies with the eyes of a fish, things become more complicated.

Fish can see colors - this is a fact. But in regard to dry flies, for example, color is by no means as important as was once thought by fly tiers and flyfishermen. The fish see a fly from below, outlined against the sky in backlight, so they can hardly distinguish between different color tones. In practice, it often turns out that we can do quite well with a small range of dry flies in a few colors.

Down at the water, of course, the fish can study our wet flies. Still, exact colour nuances are seldom decisive. This is because there are large individual differences between natural insects. For instance, nymphs which have to molt their skins are very dark, while those which have just done so are very light. Thus the fish see both dark and light insects at the same time, which means that they are not fastidious about exact colors. After all, they only want something to eat!

Colourful flies can be attractive

When we speak of colors and fish, we must remember that colours above the water surface are not the same thing as colours under the surface. The water absorbs some of the light which enters it. The murkier the water, the less light can get in, and the less significance a fly's colors have. We should also keep in mind that red is the color which fades soonest, and blue is the color that penetrates deepest. The red part of the visible spectrum is least energetic, and blue is most energetic. If you need a visible fly in deep water, it is thus a bad idea to choose a red one, which will look black to the fish and be hard to see. Instead, choose a fly with blue or green colors - ideally with plenty of tinsel, which can reflect the little available light.

Fluorescent colors have always been of great interest to flytiers. For many of us, fluorescent flies have seemed to be something magical, which now and then can save an otherwise fruitless day of fishing. But there is nothing magical about fluorescent colors. Fluorescence is due to energetic ultraviolet light, which is invisible to us. It is the same kind of light that gives a suntan or sunburn. When ultraviolet light, which is especially predominant on gray and cloudy days, hits a fluorescent material, this is activated by the light's energy and shines with unusual strength. Consequently, fluorescent colors are most clear on dark days, although they should not be confused with phosphorescent colors, which can emit light even in darkness. If there is no light, there is no fluorescence either!

In fly patterns for salmon, particularly the so-called "egg flies", fluorescent colours have made notable progress. Here they are quite superior, although of more doubtful value in smaller flies with quieter colours. Fluorescent colours seem to have the greatest effect when they are used in flies that provoke the fish to strike - in other words, flies meant for fish on spawning migrations. But they should not be forgotten if we are fishing in the cold months, when the water contains little food. Then the fish are hungry, and not especially discerning. In such situations, a fluorescent fly can attract great attention and curiosity, yielding surprisingly good results. Later in the year, when food is abundant, fluorescent colors often lose their ability to attract strikes.

A colourful fly like the classic, eternally young "Mickey Finn" is regarded as a natural attractor - that is, a fly which draws the notice of fish with its strong colors. But it is a fly which can also be very effective during the warm months, when there is plenty of food in less bright colors. Strong red-yellow hues are, perhaps, not so impressive after all. Considering the colours of a minnow or stickleback, one can see that almost every color in the spectrum is represented. So who knows? Maybe the fish believe that a fly like "Mickey Finn" is an ordinary small fish.

The fly as a caricature

The experiment with sticklebacks showed clearly that exact imitations are not necessarily the best. Other scientific studies indicate that it can even pay to exaggerate the key stimuli. A good imitation therefore need not be a fly which most resembles the prototype. It may instead be one that overemphasizes typical characteristics of the prototype. We have to think like a caricaturist who instantly hits upon the quirks of his "victim" and exaggerates them. Then there can be no

doubt of whom the picture represents. It might be said that the caricature is more realistic than reality!

If the insect to be imitated is, for instance, a mayfly which has big wings - the fly should have extra large wings. This is actually true of the so-called "no hackle" flies, already mentioned. Usually regarded as exact imitations, they are actually faithful caricatures. Their wings, which are not veiled by any hackle, tell the fish immediately that this is a mayfly.

The classic dry fly is slowly disappearing from our flyboxes and being replaced by new, better and more durable imitations. Not least the parachute flies, whose hackle is wound around the wing root, have become popular. They are easy to tie and rest low on the water, just like the real insects. At the same time, their horizontal hackle adds extraordinary buoyancy. Moreover, the fly lands as light as a feather and always correctly on the water. This is certainly not true of normally hackled dry flies with upright wings, which readily topple over and lie down on their sides.

A mayfly's last winged stage, the spent spinner, is very easy to imitate. This again is due to the modern synthetic materials, which do not absorb water. With them, we can make the flies rest in the surface layer without using hackle. The "polywing spinners" are outstanding imitations with a particularly simple structure - a pair of long tail antennae, a polypropylene body, and a horizontal wing of poly yarn. They can hardly be simpler, and the fish love them!

All these imitations rest on the water, while the hook tip and the whole hook bend protrude down under the surface. Ultimately such a fly does not closely resemble its natural prototype. Insects do not break through the surface - they stand on it. Nevertheless, thousands of very selective fish have been tricked by our flies, despite the quite unnatural iron clump which hangs beneath the surface. This could be seen as another proof that exact imitations are not very significant for the fish's view of our flies.

There are fly tiers who make complicated "upside down" flies, with hook points and bends that do not break through the water surface. But these have never been widespread, since they are too hard to tie. As we have seen, even the most selective fish are only seldom able to appreciate our exact imitations, which are primarily for the flyfisherman's own sake!

Fish often let themselves be tricked into taking, even though the fly is really a rather clumsy imitation of natural food.

Function and movement

In the long history of flyfishing there are some examples of amazingly simple flies, so simple that it might be doubted whether they can be used for fishing at all. Frank Sawyer was showered with praise when he created his now classic Pheasant Tail, a fly that consists solely of pheasant cock tail fibers and copper wire. The latter serves partly as binding thread, and partly to weight the fly so that it can sink fast.

Sawyer had noticed that mayfly nymphs of the genus Baetis hold their legs close to the body when swimming. He therefore saw no reason to put hackle on their imitations. With sparse material he was able to contrive the right form and color, while relying on the rod end to give the fly correct movements - an "induced take" which has since become famous.

Oliver Kite, one of Sawyer's disciples, further reduced the Pheasant Tail nymph. He went so far as to use only copper wire on a bare hook, and his Bare Hook Nymph caught plenty of fish. Most of his fishing for fastidious trout took place in the English chalk streams. So much for exact imitations!

Function is a key word when it comes to flies for practical fishing - and regardless of whether they are exact imitations or fantasy flies. The fly just has to work. Dry flies must float, being tied with water-repellent materials; wet flies must sink, absorbing water so as to break through the surface tension. The latter rule is crucial for non-weighted flies: light nymphs, spiders, or wet flies made to be fished high up in the water.

The current speed also influences our choice of material and flytying style. For instance, wet flies for use in still water must be tied with soft material that can look alive and move correctly. Such flies normally fish best when they are sparsely clad. Good illustrations are the classic spiders and soft hackles - their material pulsates at the slightest excuse. Superb in this respect are flies tied with marabou feathers.

The opposite rule holds if wet flies are to be used in fast currents. Here a fly tied with soft material would soon collapse and lose its originally intended shape. One should employ stronger material like cock hackle instead of hen hackle, bucktail rather than marabou, and so on.

If the fly must reach down to fish in fairly deep water, there are two alternatives: using a sinking line to pull the fly. down, or weighting the fly and fishing it with a floating line and a long leader. Both methods have their pros and cons. With a sinking line you do not need to weight the fly, which thus behaves more lively in the water. But when fishing nymphs upstream with a floating line, there is only one solution: weighted flies. Then, of course, you must remember that heavy flies are dead flies with no essential life. In sum, clear limits exist to how much the fly can be weighted without hurting its ability to catch fish. The important thing is always to tie it with soft and vital material.

Recently we have acquired fast-sinking leaders, provided with built-in weights. They allow use of a floating line and non-weighted flies. The leader enables the fly to come down to the fish anyway, while also presenting it with a light and lively fly.

From the casting viewpoint, there are definite limits to how heavy a fly can be. Strong fly lines can carry heavy flies better than light flies, but every line obviously has its limitations. Big, densely hackled dry flies create a lot of air resistance and need relatively strong lines to be laid out against the wind. This is familiar to salmon fishermen who try their luck with big dry flies of the Wulff type. But light flies can also be very heavy. Good examples are the "zonkers" and "puppies" tied with thin strips of rabbit fur. The latter have an amazing ability to absorb water, and a wet rabbit is a very heavy rabbit in terms of casting!

The flyfisherman often needs flies which are really bigger and heavier than his equipment can handle. Such is the case with imitations of many medium-size small fish, and with giant flies for huge game like tarpon and sailfish. If these flies were tied in the conventional way, they would be unduly heavy and impossible to cast.

While tying streamers and bucktails on long-shafted hooks, we usually employ short and light hooks for really large flies. They are provided with a wing which is several times longer than the hook shaft, making a fly that is very large and yet does not weigh much. To prevent the long wing from winding itself round the hook bend, it is frequently tied to the rear of the hook shaft. This is done, for instance, on special "needlefish" flies - and characteristic tarpon flies, where the long hairwing is simply replaced by saddle hackle.

Nevertheless, it is also possible to tie a tiny fly on a com-

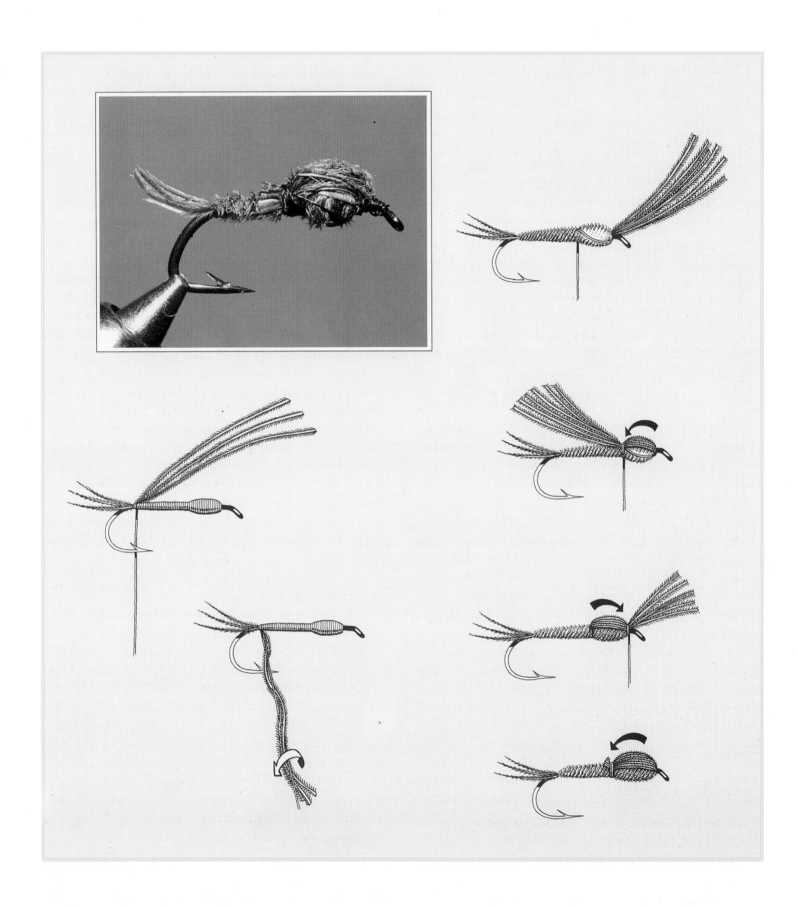

Left: The Pheasant Tail Nymph created by Frank Sawyer is as simple as it is ingenious. Having no hackle, it is tied with only copper wire and pheasant cock tail feathers.

PHEASANT TAIL NYMPH
Hook: No. 12-16
Tail: three fibers from a pheasant cock' tail feather
Body: tied and weighted with red-brorwn copper wire, using pheasant cock tail feather fibers are wound forward to the head, then bent back and forth to make an ample wingcase, and finally tied to the head

paratively large hook. Not seldom, we go after big fish that need strong hooks to be played on. But the flies must be small, since they imitate small insects. Such dry flies can be tied "double", with two flies on one hook. This offers a great advantage when the fish take midges of size 18-24. There is ample room for two flies on a hook of size 16, and then you can also use a stronger leader tippet which matches the fish's size better. Imitations of individual fish eggs - "Glo Bugs" - can likewise be made small on rather large hooks, and paradoxically at no cost to their fishing ability. Here is yet another proof that fish see flies with different eyes than we fishermen do.

Adaptation to practical fishing

Flyfishermen and fly tiers are committed, creative people who work continually to keep their hobbies progressing. Originally flyfishing had a very restricted range. The cast was short and the flies could be fished only on or just under the surface. If the fish were not there at that moment, nothing could be done about it. But today's modern, well-equipped flyfishermen want to fish everywhere and under all conditions.

Thanks to developments in gear, we can now reach farther out and deeper down than our predecessors.

When choosing a fly, you should naturally take into account its size, color and dressing, but the presentation is often what determines whether the trout will take.

Equipment

The fly line is what determines the casting weight. So it is essential that the rod be balanced against the line's weight during the cast and presentation of the fly. To obtain this balance, lines and rods are classified by a system called AFTM (American Fishing Tackle Manufacturers' Association). Which class or classes you should choose depends on the water you are fishing in - its current, required casting distance, fish size, and other factors.

Rods

Until the 1950s, nearly all fly rods were made of six glued-together segments of bamboo, with triangular cross-section. This is known as the split-cane technique. The unavoidable disadvantages of such rods were their higher weight (much higher for salmon rods), their greater demands for care and carefulness, their relatively high price and shorter lifetime. The advent of synthetic fibre rods was greeted with joy by many flyfishermen, and these rods soon dominated the market.

Carbon fiber rods began to be produced in the late 1970s. Many of us think—perhaps rightly—that their high-tech construction, low weight, fast action, and superb casting ability have revolutionized flyfishing. But it should be remembered that such rods also have drawbacks. Besides being brittle and delicate, they are fine conductors of electricity, which is a serious danger if they come into contact with high-voltage cables. Tube-built glass-fiber rods, although heavier, are thus still on the market, since these are comparatively cheap and durable, as well as often having excellent casting properties.

For technical developments have made quite good tube-built glass-fiber rods available at a fairly low price. In sum, nothing shows that an expensive rod need be better than a cheaper one.

Apart from the AFTM classification, rods are grouped according to their action—that is, how they work. Normally we distinguish between fast action, medium action, and slow action. A rod with fast action has its elasticity mainly at the top. With slow action, the entire rod works during the cast and playing. Medium action is a popular combination of these types, used in many modern fly rods.

When choosing a rod, you must know what it will be used for. The action, line class, and length are determined by the type of water and the fish's species and presumed size. One-handed fly rods are used for fishing in brooks and streams, small rivers and lakes, ponds and coastal waters Two-handed fly rods are almost exclusively for salmon fishing. Long two-handed rods make it easier to manage a lot of line in the air, but they are heavy and tiring to cast with. A short one-handed rod is convenient when the fishing water is surrounded by bushes and thickets.

The choice of rod depends on further things too. One must check that the handle, reel seat, windings and guides are of good quality and that the rod has enough spine. Generally you can control the line and fly more easily on the water, and achieve a more even casting rhythm, with a longer rod. Rods under 7 ft (2.1 m) cannot be recommended except under very special conditions. For those who need advice when choosing equipment, the following may serve as guidelines.

7.5-9.5 ft (2.2-2.9 m), AFTM class 4-6: fishing in brooks and small streams.

8-10 ft (2.4-3.0 m), AFTM class 6-8: fishing in large streams, lakes, small rivers, and for light coastal flyfishing.

10-13 ft (3.0-4.0 m), AFTM class 9-10: fishing at coasts, large lakes, and for light salmon fishing.

14-18 ft (4.3-5.5 m), AFTM class 10-12: heavy coastal and salmon fishing.

Lines

As the fly line has decisive importance for the cast and presentation of the fly, demands on lines are very high today. They must be supple, light casting, durable, and easy to feed out through the guides.

Functionally, the fly line helps with its weight in carrying out the feather-light fly. Lines are therefore grouped in twelve standard classes, on the basis of the weight of the line's first 30 ft (9 m) measured from the line tip. Higher class means greater line weight.

To make the equipment suitable for different types of fish, we have not only the AFTM system but also variations in the tapering of fly lines. This refers to the line's profile, and two main groups exist. A double-tapered line (DT) is thickest in

---

In order to cast correctly and present the fly elegantly to the fish, there must be good balance between the rod and line.

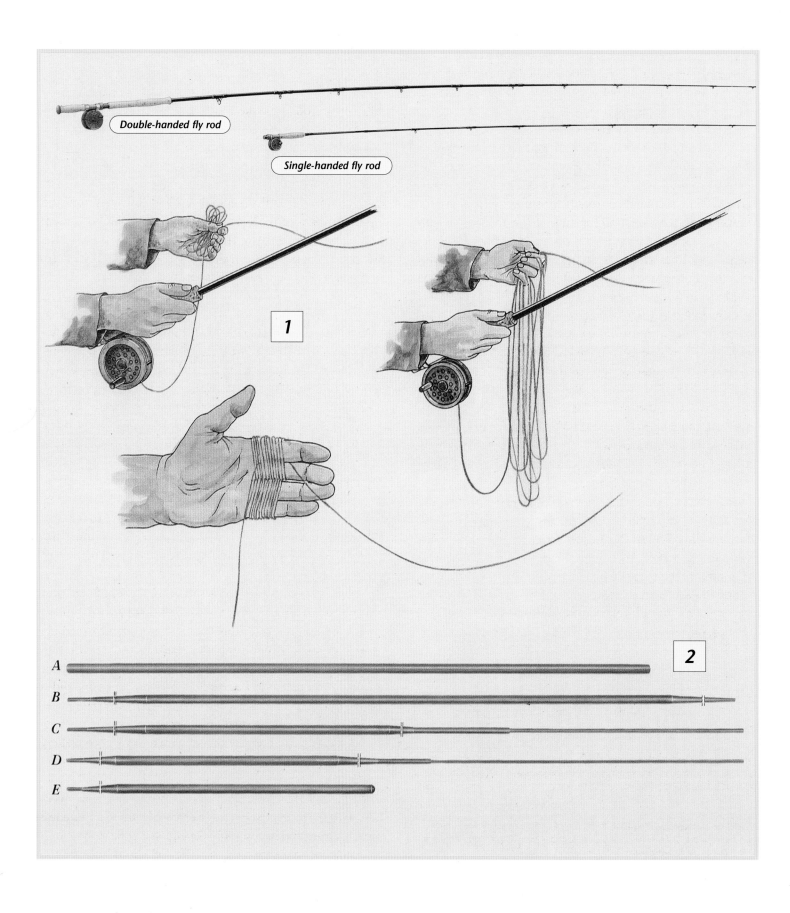

Double-handed fly rod

Single-handed fly rod

1

2

A

B

C

D

E

the middle and becomes gradually thinner toward both ends. A weight-forward line (WF), besides its tip, consists of a "belly" about 26 ft (8 m) long - where the weight is concentrated - and a long casting line.

The DT line is used most, because it allows soft and harmonious casts, which are essential for well-aimed and discreet layout of the fly. Its popularity is naturally increased by the fact that it can be turned round when one end has worn out.

The WF line is suitable primarily for situations that call for a longer cast. Depending on the kind of use, the belly length varies. Most marked and short is the belly on the "saltwater tapered" WF line, which serves especially for long casts with heavy flies in bass and saltwater fishing. The "long-belly" line (WFL) has an extremely long clump that makes it behave like a WF line in long casts, yet like a DT line in short casts. A third type of line is the "shooting taper" (ST), also called "single taper", which consists of a short clump attached in a thin casting line, and operates like a projectile when the fishing needs a really long cast.

There is also a distinction between floating and sinking lines. A floating line (F) is used in dry-fly fishing, and when fishing with nymphs or wet flies on the surface. Sinking lines (S) are required when the fish stay deep. Within these groups are also various classes. We speak mainly of slow-sinking (Intermediate), normal-sinking, fast-sinking, and extra-fast sinking lines. In addition, various sink-tip (F/S) types are on the market, and can be preferable to sinking lines - for they give full control over the floating section, and their sinking end can be adapted to the type of fishing at hand. Rapid currents obviously call for heavier (and thus more slowly sinking) line than do still waters, in reaching down to a given depth.

1. To facilitate the cast and presentation of the fly, it is necessary to control the loose line neatly. At left are shown three common ways of organizing the line as it is taken in. But the most usual method, illustrated at right, is to hold the line in loops with your line hand.

2. All lines are classified according to their profile. Shown here, respectively from the top, are: A Level line (L), B Double-taper line (DT), C Long-belly line (WFL), D Weight-forward line (WF), E Single-taper line (ST).

The line's color is frequently less important than we tend to believe. Fish are hardly frightened by a fly line even if it is very colorful, provided that the leader is long enough. On the other hand, one must keep in mind that light-colored lines are easier to see when the illumination is poor. Sinking lines, of course, do not suffer by being dark.

Fly lines should always be supplemented with a backing line, or reserve, in case a far-rushing fish takes the fly. A backing line also fills up the reel so that the fly line does not wind up in too tight turns. Such lines are made of monofilament nylon or braided Dacron. The latter is usually most expensive, but pays off in the long run since it ages well, is more durable, and tangles less than monofilament line.

Reels

The fly reel is commonly the least emphasized part of our fly-fishing equipment. A functional reel must fulfill two requirements: having enough room for backing and fly lines, as well as being able to play big fish effectively. For salmon fishing in particular, it must tolerate long and powerful runs without breaking down. Playing a hooked fish with a loose line lying on the ground is a cause of concern, with the inevitable tangle and lost fish. At least 100 m (330 ft) of backing line, in addition to the fly line, have to fit on the reel. There must be an adjustable, dependable braking system. The reel should be easy to care for, and soundly constructed with no gap between the spool and housing where the line might get stuck and damaged. Moreover, it should have easily replaceable spools so that you need not carry a reel for each line.

The most usual type of reel is doubtless the traditional one, simply built with no finery. Its handle sits right on the spool, which rotates once each time the handle is turned as the line is wound on - and in the opposite direction as the line is pulled off. When the line is drawn out, the spool is braked by means of an adjustable screw, and you can use your index finger to brake more effectively. This type of reel operates superbly when playing small fish.

Big fighting fish are best chased with a reel whose braking system is more powerful and efficient, such as a slip (clutch) brake or disc brake.

In general one should always choose high-quality reels. Besides making the fishing more enjoyable, they produce less wear on lines and have a more dependable braking system. It is also worth remembering that the reel should not be too

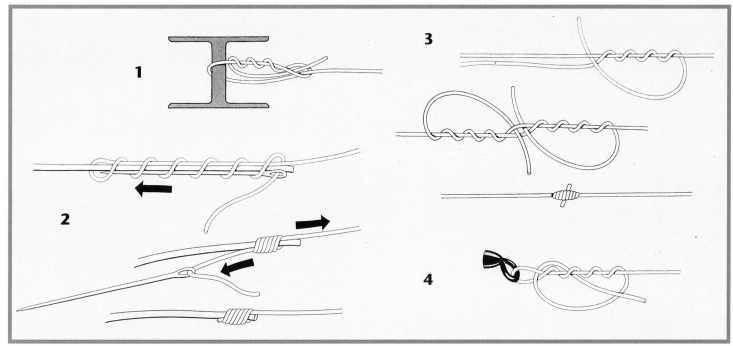

*The knots are the weakest link between fly and fisherman, so they must be durable an reliable. **1**. The spool knot (to tie the backing line on the reel spool). **2**. The nail knot (to tie the leader and backing line on the fly line). **3**. The blood knot (for tying together sections of monofil) **4**. The clinch knot (For fastening the fly and leader)*

small. It has to hold enough line and backing for the type of fishing you do. And finally, a reel for saltwater use must be corrosion-resistant.

Leaders

The leader's chief duty is to provide an even transition between the relatively thick fly line and the hook eye. A thin leader tip makes it easier to present the fly without alarming the fish, but is too readily broken off by a sizeable fish. Conversely, a thick leader tip can withstand big fish better, yet may be rather clumsy for elegant presentations.

To some extent, the leader's thickness must be adapted to the fly's size. For a thicker leader guides a big fly more accurately than an extremely thin leader tip does.

Leader tips thinner than 0.12 mm (0.005 in) should be totally avoided, and not less than 0.18 mm (0.007 in) ought

Left: A big fish has been hooked amid spectacular scenery. But will the equipment hold against the pressure?

to be used for medium-sized fish, while 0.30 mm (0.012 in) is a minimum for salmon and other true fighting fish. Large salmon that need big hooks can even call for up to 0.50 mm (0.02 in) at the tip.

The length and tapering of a leader are also important. A good rule is that it should be a little longer than the rod when fishing with dry flies and nymphs, but that 1.5-2.0 m (4.9-6.5 ft) suffices for wet-fly fishing. A leader is built up from its thicker upper end, via a more or less smoothly narrowing transitional section, to the thin tip. About 60% of its total length should consist of the strong upper part, followed by about 20% narrowing and then about 20% tip. The thickest part of the leader, which is tied or glued onto the fly line, must be around 0.5 m (1.6 ft) long with a diameter of 0.45-0.50 mm (0.02 in).

In addition, the leader has to be flexible, soft and easily cast, non-knotting, and able to keep itself stretched in and on the water. A coiled leader can really spoil your sport, not least when dry-fly fishing.

Even if there are ready-tapered leaders on sale in stores, it is not hard to tie them yourself with pieces of monofilament nylon line. The pieces in the leader material should not differ in diameter by more than 0.05 mm (0.002 in), since otherwise the knots are not as dependable.

If you choose to buy leaders ready-made, there is a great range of different types to choose among. Best are ready-tapered knotless monofilament nylon lines – and braided leaders. The latter, flexible and soft, do not curl as easily when they lie rolled up on the reel for a long period, and they give a generally good presentation of the fly.

Flies

We now come to the equipment which not only gave its name to our kind of fishing, but is the very foundation of this sport's existence - the fly. A symbol that unites the hundreds of thousands of flyfishermen all over the world, it is also a source of arguments. Some maintain that a wide choice of flies is necessary, whereas others are content with a few carefully selected flies. Many of us demand exact imitations, but equally often we consider caricatures to be what attracts the fish to strike.

Who is right or wrong in such disputes will not concern us here. Perhaps it is enough to note that our flies and fly patterns are infinitely diverse, and that flies are always a fascinating topic beside the fishing water as well as in the sportfishing stores and magazines.

Internationally, fly patterns are almost uncountable. A lot are pure fantasy flies, while many are precisely tied imitations of particular insects that may live in only one area. There is also a long list of patterns intermediate between imagination and reality. Despite this amazing variety, flies can be divided into main groups: dry flies, wet flies, nymphs, flymphs, streamers, bucktails, lures, salmon flies, and so on.

Naturally a pattern meant to imitate a certain insect has to portray its prototype in all basic respects. Yet this does not require it to be an exact copy in every detail. Only its similar characteristics need be made clear to the fish - in other words, the fly's proportions and the appearance of its body, hackle, wings, and tail must be right.

In any case, flies obviously have to fulfill their elementary functions. A wet fly should sink to the depth where fish are hunting at the time. A dry fly must be able to float high and lightly, in order to be presented as in nature. A flymph ought to remain hanging just in the surface film, or only a few centimeters under it. The purpose of a salmon fly is to somehow provoke the aggressive spawning fish to strike. And so on...!

Accessories

The equipment described until now is an absolute prerequisite for effective flyfishing. But there are quite a lot of items that can make your fishing easier and pleasanter, although not essential to its success.

Clothing should first and foremost be roomy, comfortable and rugged. It ought to give the fisherman proper camouflage, so as not to frighten the fish unnecessarily. Moreover, it should withstand rain and wind, as well as having plenty of pockets to help you organize your fishing adventures.

A fly vest is probably the most common piece of clothing. Its pockets must be practical and accessible. Before investing in a vest, though, you should check that the

Right: In addition to the basic equipment, a lot of useful accessories can make the fishing both easier and more fun.

fasteners – they must never be allowed to damage the hook point!

Leaders and their materials, too, must be stored so that they are not damaged. If you tie your own leaders, a dispenser is preferable to loose spools, but it must have room for at least five different sizes and the lines should be able to feed without tangling.

Your fly vest or equivalent apparel should also contain a sharp pair of scissors or nail-clippers for purposes such as cutting leader stubs and dressing knots or flies. A sharp knife is necessary for slaughtering and cleaning. Substances that increase the buoyancy of dry flies and floating lines are further examples of essential accessories. A small rotatable lamp which can easily be attached to a jacket or vest is indispensable for flyfishing at night if you want to have a fair chance of switching flies, tying leaders, and other work that needs some light. Scales and a measuring tape, flat-nosed pliers, a hook-sharpener, line grease, and a line basket can be added to complete the picture of a well- equipped flyfisherman.

Those who do not practice "catch and release" fishing, or , land their fish by hand, often need a deep and preferably collapsible landing net, or one with extension handle. And if you fish much from overgrown shores, a variant is a small collapsible landing net that can be carried in a quiver. Short-shafted, wooden framed landing-nets are good when wading, while long-shafted landing nets are more all-round and serve excellently for fishing from low or high shores as well as from boats. The inexperienced salmon fisherman who does not want to risk losing his "dream salmon" when grabbing it by the tail will need a tailer or gaff.

Basic accessories also include some sort of eye-protection. A gust of wind, or a wrong move of the rod, can easily send the fly on a dangerous course and, at worst, into your eye. Ordinary glasses or sunglasses are a cheap guard against permanent eye damage. A clear advantage of Polaroid glasses is that they filter out the sunlight reflected from the water surface, and thus increase your chances of seeing what swims under it.

pockets will really hold fly boxes and are not so shallow that the contents fall out.

Fly boxes ought to float. A box is easily dropped and, if this happens over deep water, a sinking box can be lost forever. Besides, a good fly box should be clearly arranged and must provide maximum protection for the flies and hooks. Dry flies are best kept in boxes with separate compartments that can be opened and sealed simply, or else in spacious boxes where the flies are fastened in foam-rubber bands. Wet flies are less delicate and can thus do well in relatively flat boxes. The same is true of nymphs, streamers and salmon flies, where it is most important that hooks and barbs do not lose their sharpness. We should therefore be very careful with metal clamps and similar

A fishing hat is not only symbolic of fishing success. It also helps to protect the face and eyes from flies that change course during the cast. Besides a broad brim or a screen, the hat should have a deep shape and cover as much as possible of your face, ears and neck.

Sooner or later, one finds that many fine fishing spots cannot be reached without a pair of thigh or body waders. Which of these you choose depends mainly on the water depth. Body waders can take you into relatively deep areas, but they are clumsy to wear in shallow water or on land, and uncomfortable condensation easily forms inside them. Thigh waders are lighter to walk and move in, but limit the depth of water you can enter.

Body waders made of neoprene have many advantages over the "old" rubber type. They are convenient to wade in, provide fine insulation against cold water, and can easily be repaired by the waterside. A drawback is still their expensiveness.

Whether you use thigh or body waders, and whatever the material, certain demands should be placed on their soles. These must primarily be non-slip. The bottoms should be covered with felt or matting, to prevent your slipping on stones and perhaps being taken by the current. Another advantage of silent materials like felt is that they do not scare shy fish as readily when you wade.

As an aid, some kind of wading staff should be used. You can easily make one from any stable length of wood. The important thing is that it does not bend even under-heavy force. For this reason, be careful when buying a staff that can be disassembled, as it must be able to support a hard leaning body. A good wading staff should also have an eye or other device where you can attach, for example, a rubber cord to keep the staff from drifting away with the current if you happen to let go of it. Ideally it ought to have a sound muffling "shoe", for instance of rubber, as the fish are then not frightened so easily.

Another helpmate for fishing at some distance from shore is a float-ring (belly-boat). This is used almost exclusively in still or very slow waters. You then have every advantage of a boat, and it is a lot easier to transport and launch. But obviously greater care is needed with sharp objects in a belly-boat. A puncture while far out in a lake can be disastrous. One should therefore always make sure that the belly-boat has a two-chamber system.

Casting with a single-handed rod

As mentioned earlier the casting weight is determined by the fly line. In other words, the fly is transported out to the fish by means of the line. This undoubtedly looks much harder than it is in practice when the art has been learned. For a beginner, getting the fly and line out while avoiding nearby trees and bushes is almost impossible. Yet only a few hours of intensive training are usually required in order to grasp the basics so well that at least ten meters of line can be cast with no real trouble.

To achieve long casts and complete precise presentations, you often have to spend a long time on different fishing waters. But the fact is that fishing can be effective even with

Above: A fishing hat protects the face and eyes from flies that change course during the cast.
Fly box ought to float – a sinking box can be lost forever.

Right: Long casts are not necessary for catching fish with a single-handed rod.

Overhead cast

relatively short casts. Long casts are not at all necessary for catching fish, especially in small waterways. It is, however, quite essential to learn correct presentation of the fly, whether you are casting long or short.

Practice and more practice: this is the recipe for learning how to cast harmoniously. A skilful instructor is certainly worth having, but not a prerequisite - the best teacher of casting is the process of fishing itself.

Basic casting technique

When learning to cast flies, you should start in a place with room for the back cast. Many people begin to practice on a grass lawn, but the best location is a lakeside, since laying the line on the water is an essential part of many casts. For the line's friction against the water - which cannot be obtained on a lawn - helps to build up the action in the rod. Certain casts, such as the roll and switch cast, are just impossible to perform except on water.

It is simplest to begin with a single-handed rod of 8-9 ft (2.4-2.7 m). To protect the tip of the fly line, a piece of leader should always be tied farthest out. Moreover, tie on a fly with its barb nipped off. The fly helps to stretch the leader tip, giving better control over the final phase of the cast.

A good cast is based on harmony between the line, rod, and casting arm. One common beginner's mistake is to force the cast, particularly the forward cast. Many are also afraid that the line will hit the ground, and do not wait until the back cast has really stretched out. As a result, the cast collapses and the line falls in a heap. To avoid this and acquire the right rhythm, you should turn your head during the back cast, watching how the line moves and when it has stretched out completely. Only then does the time come to start the forward cast. Calm, smooth movements are the essence of becoming a good caster.

Here we shall briefly describe the traditional casts and their variants. But the continual progress of developments in equipment makes it likely that opportunities will arise in the future for learning new types of cast - tested and adapted to suit modern rods, reels, lines and leaders.

The overhead cast

This is to be recommended as the basic cast. Before beginning the cast itself, pull 6-8 m (20-26 ft) of line from the reel and lay it out on the water. Hold the rod handle with your casting hand just in front of the reel and your thumb point-

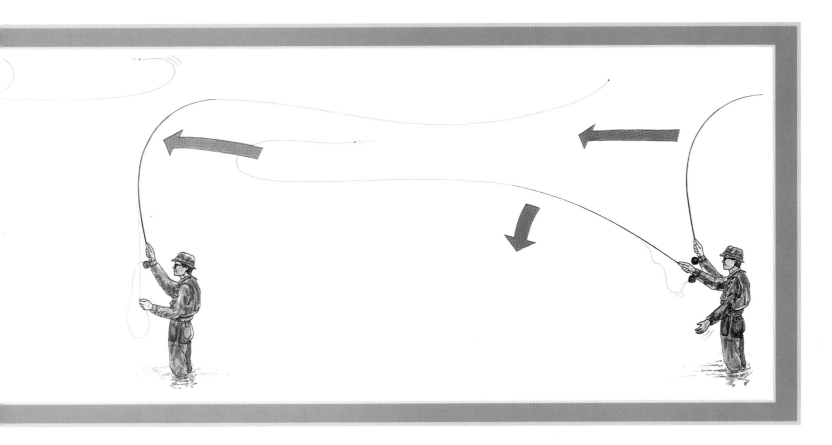

ing toward the rod top. Take the line in your other hand, held at waist height. Stand relaxed with the rod top pointing slightly downward.

Lift the rod upward with a strong but smooth movement. Once it is vertical, stop the back cast. Wait till the line is lifted and stretched out backward. When you feel the outstretched line's weight in the rod top, it is time to start the forward cast by moving the rod forward to a horizontal position - smoothly but sharply. The line now rolls forward over the rod tip and stretches out before you. Make sure that the line hand always follows the rod's movements.

The next step is to try holding the line in the air, without it collapsing on either the backward or forward cast. These air-casts are made by stopping the rod, during the forward cast, in a position pointing obliquely upward. When the line has rolled forward over the rod tip and is nearly stretched out, the rod is moved backward in a new back cast. The line now flies back and stretches out, whereupon you start a new forward cast. Once this can be done without letting the line touch the ground, you have mastered the air-cast as well.

Achieving perfect coordination requires some training and many failed attempts. But when you can keep 8-10 m (26-33

ft) in the air with no trouble, practical fishing can begin. At first, you should choose a shore area with space behind you, so that the back cast meets no obstacles. Despite this precaution, you can expect the fly to get caught occasionally on branches and bushes.

Having learned to cast 8-10 meters at the water, you can increase the amount of line in the air by a few metres each time. Hold the loose line in one hand and, when the accelerating backward-and-forward cast has added more energy, release the reserve line in a forward cast. Now the loose line shoots out through the guides to join the airborne line. This step, too, calls for exact coordination which is acquired only through much expert training. Eventually, you can thus lengthen the cast according to your ability, meter by meter.

Shooting out the line in this way is also useful when presenting the fly - not least in fishing with shoot-lines and certain other types of belly-lines, as well as in dry-fly fishing.

A variant of the overhead cast is the side cast. This horizontal, half-high movement follows the rule that a cast should be stretched out where there is enough space. It comes in handy when, for example, fishing on overgrown waterways with limited free space.

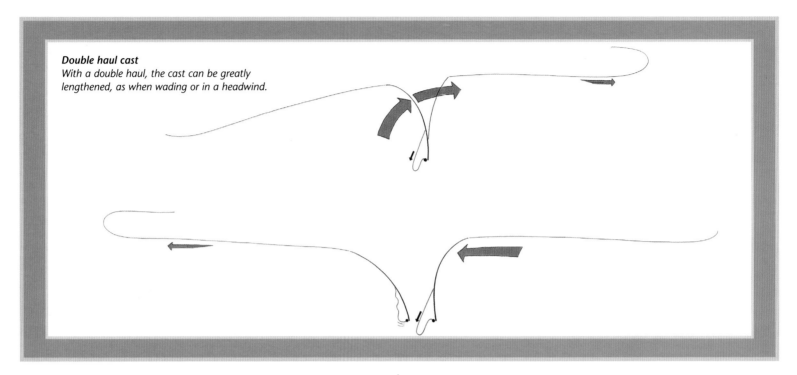

Double haul cast
With a double haul, the cast can be greatly lengthened, as when wading or in a headwind.

The double haul cast

Although on most waters we can manage with casting lengths of 10-15 m (33-50 ft), longer casts can be necessary in order to increase the chances of a catch, for instance when fishing in lakes. Even while wading, with the line almost nudging the water surface as you cast backward and forward, the technique of a double haul is very useful, since the cast easily collapses if the line touches the water.

A double haul means that you draw the fly line downward with your free line hand during both the backward and forward casts, thus increasing the line's speed and force. Begin with a strong downward haul at the very beginning of the back cast, and then complete it as usual. Just when the forward cast is to begin, make a new haul with the line hand, then release the line when the casting weight is greatest. The loose line will shoot out in the last phase of the cast.

This variant can lengthen the cast by 3-5 m (10-16 ft), but it demands exact coordination between the rod hand and line hand. Since the cast must be calm and harmonious, you should be a relatively good caster before starting to practice it.

Once the double haul is mastered, you can easily feed out a rather long line with some air-casts and finally shoot out the line by 3-5 meters. The double haul's increased line speed can be essential when you are fishing in a powerful headwind and when you need to cast far.

The serpentine cast

This cast is employed primarily in dry-fly fishing when the fly has to drift evenly without drag, even if the current is erratic. Your line hand must hold a certain amount of loose line that can be shot out in the forward cast. At the same time as the fly line shoots out, the rod top is moved rapidly forward and backward, parallel to the water surface. Thus the line lands in big curves on the water. The dry fly will gain a little extra time in order to float freely, before the fly line stretches out in the water and the fly begins to straggle. To lengthen the drift, you can also flick the rod top while releasing a little loose line, which glides out through the rod rings and adds to the line already lying on the water. This way of lengthening a cast can, of course, be used in combination with all casting variants, so that the fly will follow the current freely.

The roll cast

A roll (or switch) cast is used in fishing areas where a back cast is quite impossible to carry out. You can then certainly not cast as far, but with some training a fair length can be laid out.

About 5-6 m (16-20 ft) of line should lie stretched in front of the rod tip. Then the rod is lifted until vertical. Once the line hangs in a curve next to the fisherman, it is cast forward by means of an accelerating whip action upward, forward and

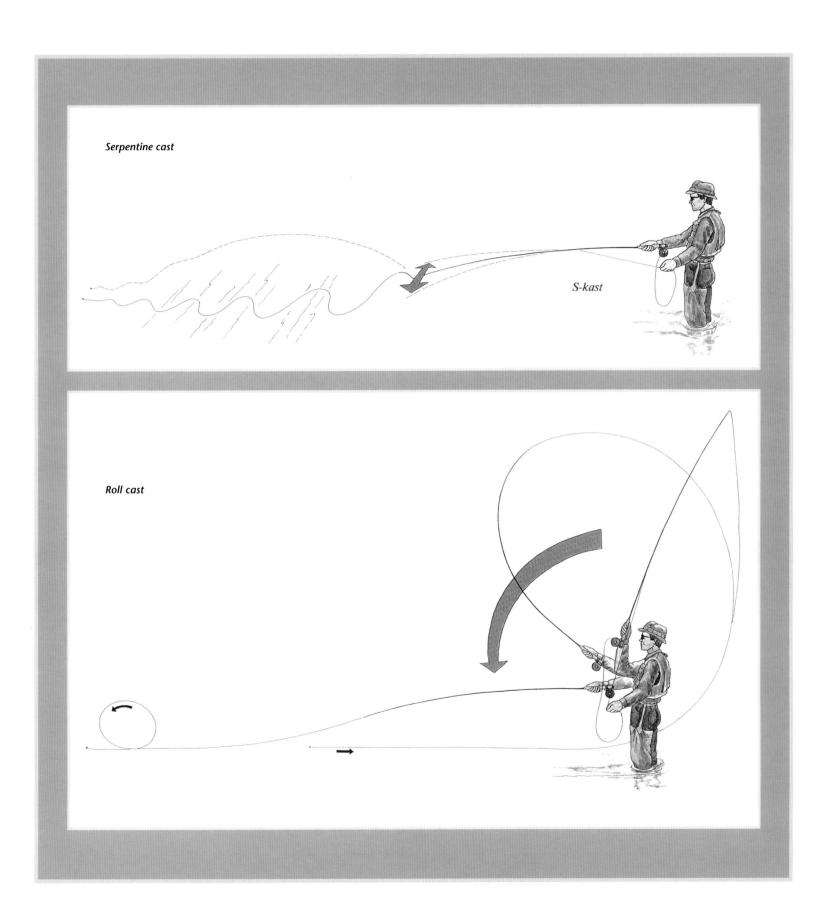

Serpentine cast

S-kast

Roll cast

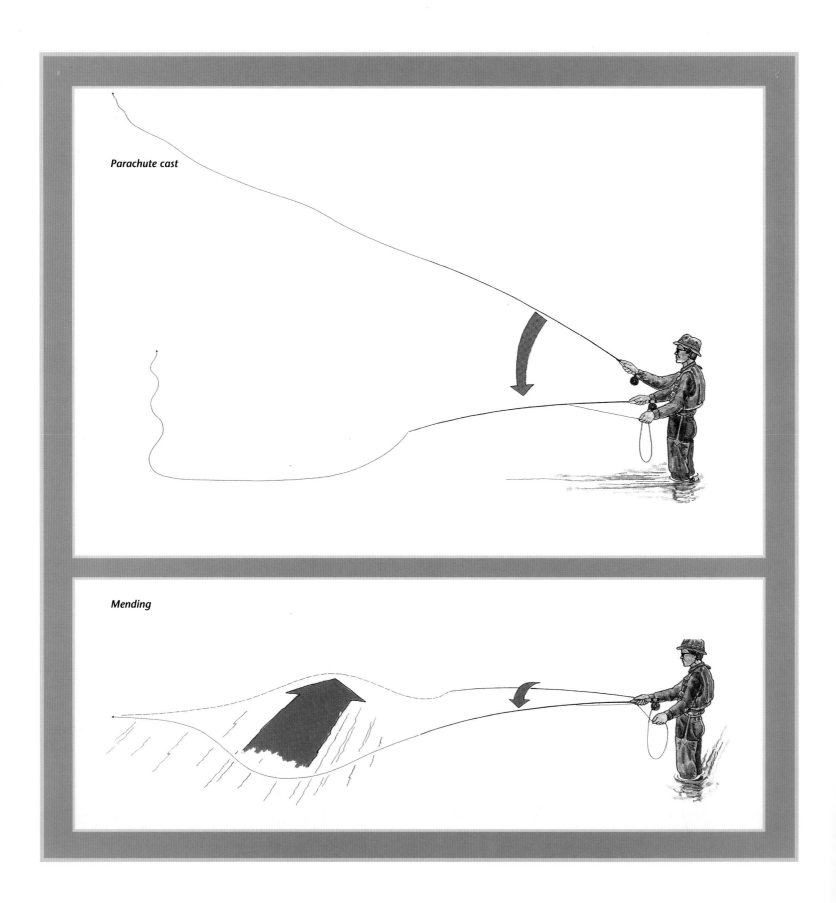

Parachute cast

Mending

then downward. The line rolls out on the water and the fly lands. By pulling out more loose line and repeating the roll cast a few times, the casting length can be increased to more than 10 m (33 ft).

One can also combine the roll cast with other casts, such as the side cast, for effective results in many situations.

The parachute cast

The difference between a serpentine cast and a parachute cast is that, in the latter, you stop the rod top during the forward cast when it is pointing obliquely upward. The line then shoots away in that direction and stretches out at the same height as the rod top. Then you lower the rod, and the fly jerks back a little before landing with the leader in curves. If the cast is done correctly, the fly, leader, and line end will land after the fly line's rear portion. And the fly can drift somewhat farther downstream without dragging.

Mending

The purpose of mending is to prevent flies from dragging or being hindered in their natural drift when the current takes the fly line and drags it along in big curves. You simply float the fly line some distance upstream by mending it, without affecting the leader tip or the fly. Mending is a cast-like movement parallel to the water surface in the current direction. If it is properly performed, the fly line will be laid in a gentle upstream curve. Thus you can considerably lengthen the natural drift-in principle, until the cast is completely fished out and the fly line ends straight downstream parallel to the shore. When fishing for salmon, it is sometimes necessary to mend downstream in order to increase the fly's speed.

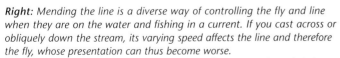

Right: Mending the line is a diverse way of controlling the fly and line when they are on the water and fishing in a current. If you cast across or obliquely down the stream, its varying speed affects the line and therefore the fly, whose presentation can thus become worse.

Shown here, the line is mended upstream, by moving the rod tip in a semicircle straight upward and upstream.

Casting with a double-handed rod

Fishing is generally the same with a double-handed rod as with a single-handed rod, but it can be very arduous and energy demanding because a double-handed rod is longer and heavier. Consequently, a couple of variant casts have been developed specially for this kind of fishing. Perhaps the best known is the Spey cast, which works well in nearly all situations if done right. This cast requires relatively little strength, is effective even in a wind, and does not need any space for a back cast. Moreover, it produces no knots on the leader - which are common in, for example, the traditional overhead cast.

The overhead cast

Casting with a double-handed rod differs in several respects from its single-handed counterpart. But the overhead cast is essentially built up in the same way. Obviously it also has the same weaknesses: you need a lot of space for the back cast, the leader can easily become knotted, and you often have to do an excessive number of blind casts which can be tiresome with a heavy double-handed rod. The aim should be to do only one back cast and then lay out the fly.

The underhand cast

The hard work of fishing with long double-handed rods is made much more comfortable by modern, light rods of carbon fiber and/or boron. However, it is still important to learn energy-saving methods of casting.

An underhand cast is not only elegant, but also offers the opportunity of fishing for a long interval without getting tired. In addition, this restful cast is quite effective. Using a back cast, the line is brought under the rod in front of you. When the rod is pointing obliquely backward, the movement stops and the forward cast begins. At this moment the line should not be fully outstretched backward. It must be given the most energy when the rod tip is pointing obliquely forward. With a single air-cast, the line can be laid out nicely in this way.

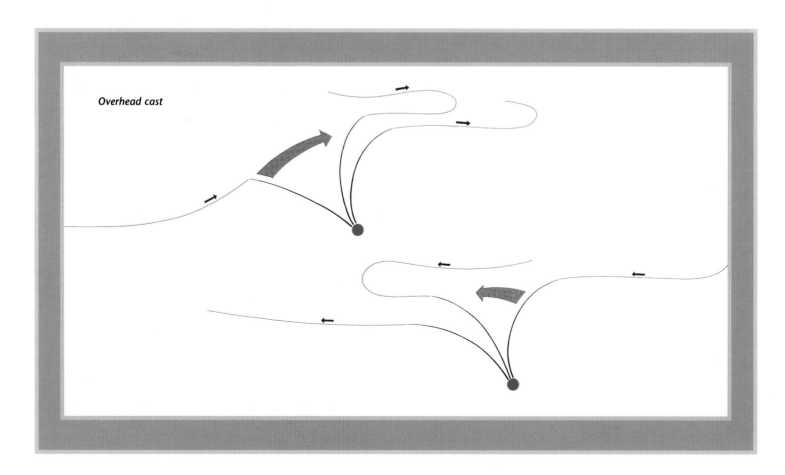

Overhead cast

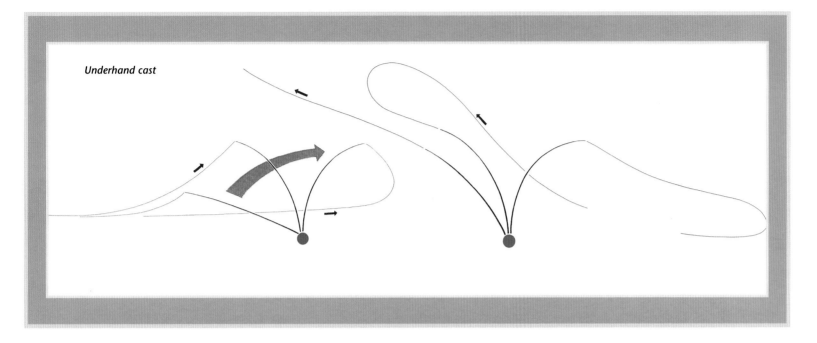

Underhand cast

The switch cast

As its name implies, the switch (roll) cast means that the fly line is rolled out onto the water. This cast comes into use mainly on shores with limited space for back casting. It must also be mastered if you want to learn the effective Spey cast properly.

Your rod should have a good spine. During the back cast, it is brought calmly to a position pointing obliquely backward. Now the line must hang in a soft curve alongside you. In the forward cast, the rod is strongly accelerated forward and downward until it is parallel to the water surface. The line then rolls out across the water in a beautiful bow.

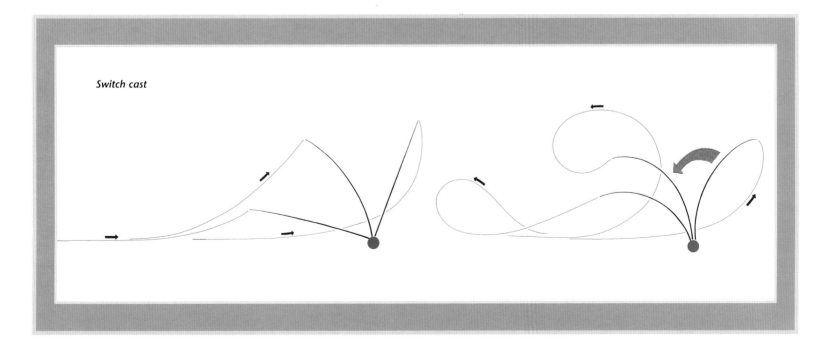

Switch cast

The Spey cast

Like the roll cast, this cast is used on shores where vegetation restricts the possibility of casting backward. It also resembles the roll cast in other essential respects. The important thing is that the fly should be placed in the right position before the forward cast, so that the hook does not catch on the line when the casting direction is changed by 45°. Hence, the fly is often allowed to float straight downstream with the current. A "double" Spey cast exists, too, but here we shall concentrate on the single Spey cast, as it also provides the basis for the double one.

Just as with the roll cast, you lift the line from the water by moving the rod to a position pointing obliquely backward. With an accelerating underhand cast, the line is brought backward and upstream on your outer side. But not so much that the fly line's tip soars into the air- it should nudge the water surface, thus adding force to the forward cast. The greatest transfer of energy should occur when the rod is pointing obliquely forward. However, the rod's own action does most of the work. This cast, as well, must be performed gently and harmoniously in a single sweep. It is easiest to carry out with a floating DT line.

The Spey cast has several advantages. It permits a long cast even where the back cast is difficult because of dense shore vegetation; it is not affected much by strong wind; and it demands relatively little muscle power during the actual cast.

Spey cast

Flyfishing in still waters

Rapidly expanding numbers of flyfishermen are well on the way to charting all the earth's flowing waters. While crowding increases on the "classic" streams - of which the sport's pioneers spoke so enthusiastically in books that remain highly readable - the destinations of flyfishermen are becoming distant and exotic.

Unknown territory in the flyfishing world is thus getting scarce and, if Glasnost applies to us too, we may soon learn whether it is true that giant trout exist in the Soviet rivers running north to the Arctic, where fish of 30-40 kg (66-88 lb) are rumored.

But for those who stay around home, fish have thinned out in the currents of many countries, despite improved management of their habitats. Flyfishing continues to grow anyway, and its practitioners demand the opportunity to fish at a reasonable cost, which also means at a reasonable distance from their origins.

Until now, they have often been satisfied, although most flyfishermen live in urban industrial regions. However, things would be far more difficult if we insisted on pursuing the sport in its "classic" form, along streams with natural stocks of salmonoid fish. The prerequisite has been, and is, that we take advantage of a vast reservoir of fish in our lakes.

Lakes offer virtually unlimited possibilities for flyfishing, apart from the insistence by a majority of us that our fish should have adipose fins. In Scandinavia alone, for example, there are thousands of lakes with more or less intact stocks of salmonoids, and further thousands whose water quality makes stocking especially of rainbow trout a meaningful, and indeed profitable, enterprise.

This is a revival of lake flyfishing in the sense that our pioneers, at least in Great Britain, sometimes fished for both sea trout and ordinary brown trout. At any rate, it is the best explanation for the fast growth of flyfishing. In Great Britain, where many reservoirs have been built to collect fresh water for urban needs, a kind of revolution is in the air: reservoirs are stocked with fish and provide recreation for tens of thousands of new and old flyfishermen.

Put-and-take fakes have enabled flyfishing to go on developing in several parts of Europe. Most of the numerous young people who try flyfishing as a hobby gain their first experience on these still waters. And they are right to do so, since one ought to get through the commonest beginner's mistakes before making an attempt on wild waterways, where the fishing is usually much harder.

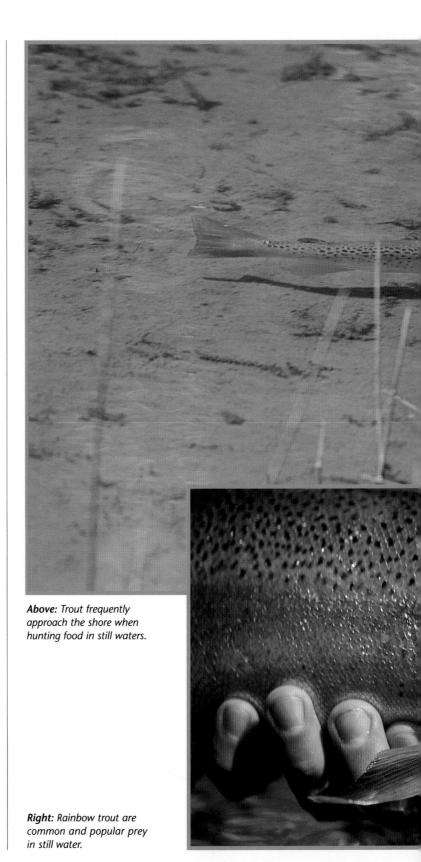

Above: Trout frequently approach the shore when hunting food in still waters.

Right: Rainbow trout are common and popular prey in still water.

You cannot learn to flyfish by reading a book about it. But a good book can provide facts and suggest experiments that pay off. Unfortunately books about lake flyfishing are rare, at least in comparison to those about fish in flowing waters. Once you do manage to learn the correct tactics and strategy for flyfishing, though, you can often catch a lot of fish - and big fish at that.

Reading the waters

People who grow up in districts with abundant waterways soon learn to "read" them as fish do. The fish are where the food is, and the most, as well as largest, fish can be found where the underwater menu is marvelous. Here they stand in the current, or scour a small area, since they need not waste energy on hunting. The current brings them all they can eat, like an endless conveyor belt in a free restaurant.

As a result, some places in a river or stream are better than others - especially where several waterways run together, or where backwaters form that concentrate the food. Adult grayling and whitefish, for instance, assemble there, at times in great schools; and it is there that the flyfisherman encounters the biggest fish. Such trout are usually solitary, because trout defend their territory with zeal and they seldom allow smaller competitors to eat at the same table.

These optimum feeding spots amount to only a fraction of the water surface's total area. Certainly much of a productive waterway can provide food during several months of the year, but not enough of it to support big fish, let alone entire schools of adult fish. However, this is sufficient for small fish until they reach a size adequate to compete for the better feeding places.

Thus, a flyfisherman must be able to "read" a waterway for the movements and color changes that show where its special fish-food resources lie. At times when plenty of insects are hatching, the fish themselves reveal these places by rising greedily. If they do not rise, it can be worth the trouble to watch such places discreetly, as any fish there will give themselves away sooner or later.

Another means of detection is to test a place with a "tempter", one of the favorite dry flies or nymphs that usually yield results even when fish are not rising. Most flyfishermen have, or eventually acquire, a little hoard of such helpmates, which can provoke a fish to strike even if it is temporarily selective - that is, bent on eating a special kind of insect in a particular stage of life.

An experienced flyfisherman has learned his "reading" and soon finds where the fish are feeding, whether or not he is on familiar waters. This is not difficult, at least on small streams. Although it may happen that only small fish take the fly, this does not mean that the water has been read wrongly. Sometimes food is scarce even in the right place - and then the big fish, especially when they are fully grown trout, go back to their hideouts in deep holes under the main current or the root systems of shore trees.

The large fish in streams are almost perfect economic machines. Hunting has to pay off, in other words to yield more food energy than the hunting consumes. When not enough food exists at their favorite feeding places, the fish do not eat at all, preferring to wait. But when the menu improves, they show up instantly to chase away smaller fish and feast on the goodies brought by the current.

This behavior is notably typical of large trout, which - during intense insect hatchings - can be seen "swinging" at the surface as they eat: first a part of the head appears, then the back, and finally the upper tail fin, a sequence repeated three or four times in a row. Having risen to the surface when insects are dense, they take an insect at every "swing". After eating as many as five insects, they glide back to the bottom and soon rise again. For a big trout, it is not economical to rise for a single insect: several must be eaten each time to restore the energy that is spent.

Moreover, this behavior gives the flyfisherman his chance of catching a "dream fish". Such a trout rises so regularly that its return to the surface can often be predicted exactly. A "swinging" trout is also virtually blind, as the movement restricts its field of vision, allowing the fisher man to wade within easy casting distance.

Yet the "reading" of water, and the fishing tactics used at clearly identifiable feeding places, are peculiar to waterways where we can find fish at the same places year after year - and can even catch the same individual fish more than once, at least in the case of trout. For trout are able to spend their whole lives in one limited section of a stream, as long as it contains plenty of food.

In the still waters of lakes, meres and ponds, the same fish species have other habits. Here they seldom meet currents that transport food to particular feeding places. Certain areas do frequently produce abundant fish food, but the fish have to locate those areas at the moments when the supply is greatest.

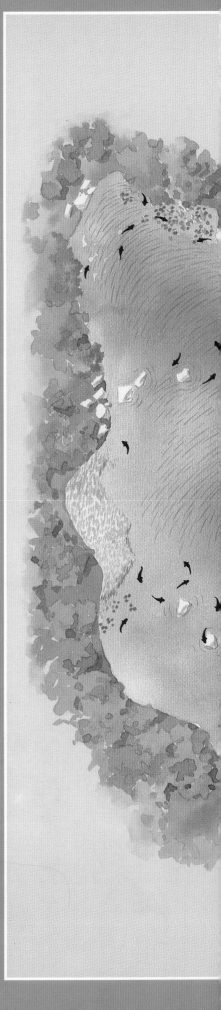

Even for a seasoned flyfisherman, it is sometimes very hard to tell where the fish are. But just as in running waters, there are special places where, for various reasons, fish can be found: for example, at stony banks and underwater beds, vegetated shores, lee edges, deep edges, coves, islets, channels, promontories, inlets and outlets.

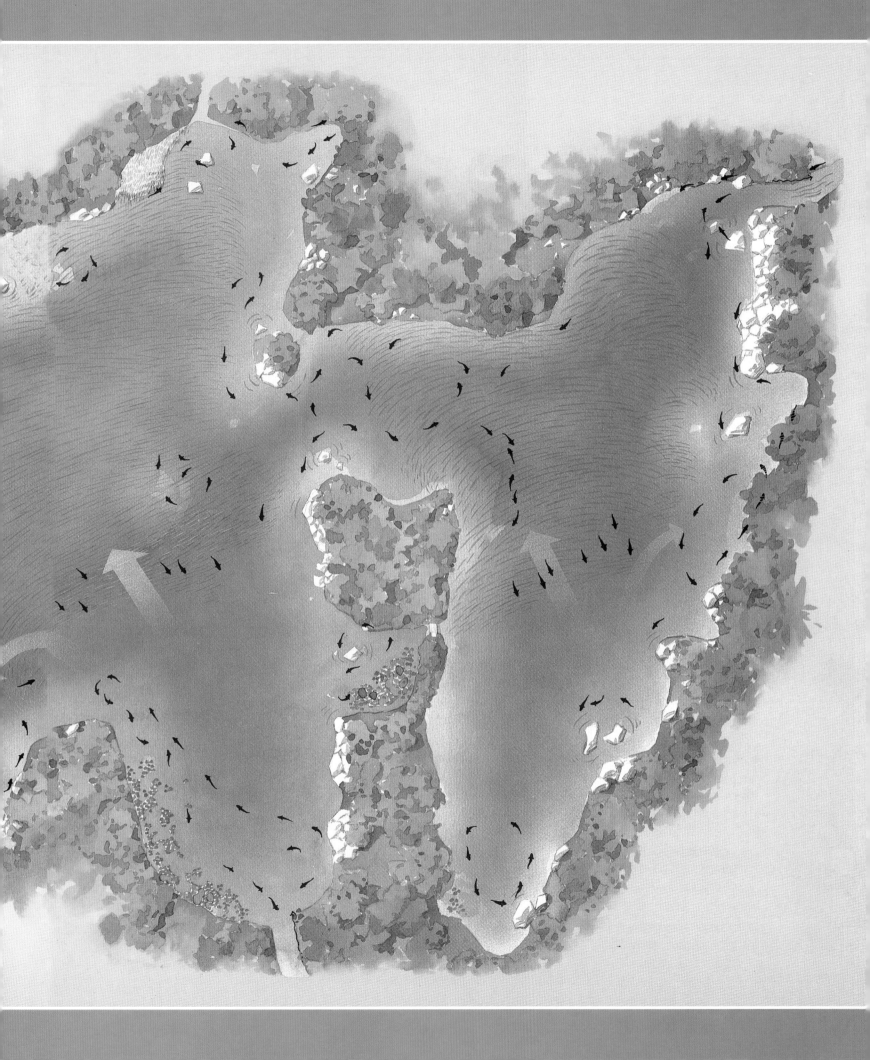

Still-water flyfishing equipment

Something like ninety percent of all the fish caught on flies in streams are taken at a distance of 8-12 m (25-40 ft). Farther away than that, it is much harder to see what the fish is doing with the fly, and more difficult to hook the fish. At over 20 m (65 ft), we seldom succeed.

When fishing in still water, it is much more important to be able to cast far, especially with nymphs and streamers. These depend on the fly being kept in motion all the time, which means that the line is straight.

There is also something that makes longer casts profitable when fishing in still waters: the mere fact that the water is still, and occasionally quite smooth. It is then difficult to get near the fish without frightening them. Currents make it easier for the flyfisherman to hide - he can sneak or wade very close, even to large shy fish, by exploiting the disturbed water's camouflage and the "dead angle" of the fish's field of vision.

Water troubled by waves and gusts of wind can also be used to advantage when fishing in still water, but the "dead angle" seldom can be. For the fish are moving and it is rarely possible to sneak up on them from behind.

Still-water fishing therefore imposes certain demands on the flyfisherman's casting ability, and consequently on the equipment. A long rod of 9.5-10 ft (around 3 m) is adequate, able to cast a light line such as a WF 5 when the wind permits, as it often does when fishing in still water. With a long rod and a light WF line, you can cast farther than 20 m (66 ft) if necessary, yet fish discreetly - which is much more important on calm lake water than in the rough waters of streams.

Another reason for choosing a long rod is that many lakes, not least in the Scandinavian mountains, are relatively shallow and call for wading. But wading at any depth makes it hard to cast with a short rod - the fly tends to hit the water during the back cast, so that the forward cast scarcely resembles what you intended.

Body waders should reach up to the armpits. Thigh waders, which reach only to the crotch, are used less often and only in calm stream waters. Otherwise you might miss many fine fishing opportunities by being unable to wade far enough out to reach underwater precipices which fish usually prefer, notably the tricky and very easily frightened Arctic char.

When fishing in lakes, a long rod and light line are preferable. With this combination, you cast long and also present the fly discreetly, as is often necessary in order to induce the fish to take. A landing net, of course, makes it easier to land the fish calmly and securely when the fight is ending

In regard to other details of equipment, besides flies for still-water fishing, you should be warned against the advice in many fishing books about the length of the backing line More than 50 m (165 ft) may be needed at times, and to lose your first four-pound trout because the backing line is too short would be infuriating, to say the least. A proper length is 100 m (330 ft), though there are times when even that can be too short.

Fishing at the right depth

Sinking lines are used more often in still waters than in currents, except for salmon and sea-trout fishing in deep, cold rivers. There are many situations, and many lakes, where the fly must be fished deep in order to make any contact with the fish. This is especially true in the early part of the season, when the water is cold and the fish seek food on the bottom. But frequently also during the season's warm periods, the fish become hard to reach, fleeing from the warm surface water to the cool bottom-layer. Then, too, a sinking line can come in handy.

However, even if the fly must descend to, say, 10 m (33 ft), it is wise to avoid fast-sinking lines. They maximize the risk of a very troublesome bottom-snag. A better method is to join a floating level-line of class 3 or 4 with a heavy "belly" of only 7-8 m (23-26 ft) made from a sinking line in the middle class range.

Such a line arrangement means that the sinking-line belly's tip will go deepest. The floating shooting line lifts the belly's other end, so that the belly cannot get snagged except, perhaps, at the tip. But nine times out of ten, only the fly gets caught and, if it does not pull loose, you can quickly tie a new one on the leader tip - which, if made properly, has broken nearest to the fly.

For deep fishing, a sinking belly in the middle class range is a good choice. It descends fast enough - that is, it stays at the same depth if you take home the line at the most suitable rate for fishing with nymphs or with small streamers. A fast-sinking belly (or the type called super-fast sinking) has to be pulled home too quickly to avoid a bottom snag, and then the fly will attract fewer fish.

But for moderate depths, say 2-3 m (6-10 ft), a sink-tip line is recommended. It has a sinking tip 3-5 m (10-16 ft) long, while the rest floats. Such a line is often a bit tricky to cast with - the heavier tip "slings" in the cast - and an alternative is a floating line with sinking leader. Nowadays there are braided leaders, from floating to very fast-sinking, and the sinking ones yield the same results as the sink-tip line's tip. They are rather expensive, but many flyfishermen prefer them anyway.

The float ring has created new opportunities for stillwater flyfishermen to cover their waters effectively. Aided by flippers, you can move silently and calmly without scaring the fish.

One does not, after all, need to change the reel or line, but simply changes the leader to fish deep.

Even a floating line with a sinking leader can get caught during the cast. This effect seems very hard to avoid, if you want a line arrangement that protects against too many difficult bottom snags. An old trick is to put a few cloven lead shot balls on the leader to the floating line. This works well, though the shot balls sometimes fly off in their own direction during the cast!

According to an ancient sportfishing rule, the fish is usually caught either at the surface or on the bottom. The same largely applies to stillwater flyfishing, where experience tells us that 95% of the fish are caught with flies on, in, or just under the water surface - and the rest are caught by fishing as close as possible to the bottom.

Certainly there are exceptions. The most important thing, of course, is to fish so that your quarry can see the fly. A fish feeding in the bottom gravel may well rise to a fly that passes 1-2 m (3-6 ft) over its head, if only it glimpses the goodie - and so may a fish swimming at a depth of 1 m (3 ft) if it discovers an attractive dry fly. But the general rule, at the surface or on the bottom, remains a good fishing tactic.

Several other tricks make it easier for the fish to find the . fly, even if you do not hit the center of the rise-ring exactly when the fish creates it. One trick, when the fly - either wet or dry - has landed, is to wait a couple of seconds and then resolutely pull in the line by 30-40 cm (12-16 in), before taking a new pause of two or three seconds. If the fish saw the fly when it fell on or into the water, and wants to take it, the strike will usually come instantly. Otherwise the fly may have fallen in the "dead angle" behind the fish. But the fish will sense the first distinct pull, and as a rule it will turn round and take the fly like lightning.

In a word, letting the fly make noise can be profitable. A good recipe is to supplement reliable wet-fly patterns with a little Muddler head, so that the fly stays hanging in the underside of the water surface. When you carefully retrieve the fly, every little tug will form a ripple around its head – and these "bow waves" seem to attract fish, or at least enable them to detect the fly more easily.

We thus return to the subject of still-water flies. The fly is the most important piece in a flyfisherman's equipment - the only item in the collection that the fish are allowed to see, if the fisherman is handling his gear in the right way.

Flies for still water

Every rule does have an exception, and there are quite a few instances in the rule book of flyfishing. Yet on the whole, two clear differences exist between still-water flies and the flies that have been proven most effective in flowing water.

On the one hand, still-water flies are all bigger by two or four hook numbers. On the other, dry flies are predominant in flowing water, but play a secondary role in still water, where wet flies hold sway and, indeed, "lures" and streamers earn a much larger share of the credit - as reckoned in number and size of fish caught.

This contrast is hardly surprising. Most dry flies imitate mayflies, whose family has far fewer species in lakes, meres and ponds than in flowing water. Caddis flies are equally plentiful in all of these, although their species, too, are definitely fewer in still waters.

However, still waters frequently offer abundant fish food of another kind: the damselfly nymphs, water boatmen and other beetles, leeches, snails and molluses, a rich assortment of land insects such as ants, sloebugs, wasps and crane flies, as well as billions of midges in various stages of life. Not to mention, of course, a lot more fish fry - the kind of food that is often essential if trout, in particular, are to grow really big.

Stoneflies are a family which tends to be strongly represented in waterways that are clean enough, and which sometimes enables us to fish with dry flies as soon as the ice melts. In Southeast European waters like the Austrian and Yugoslav chalk streams, stoneflies may dominate the insect life during much of the season, but they do not occur at all in still waters.

These differences - and there are many more - lead rather inevitably to a choice of fly patterns only some of which are usable in both still and flowing waters, and are then also tied on hooks bigger by two to four numbers if used in still waters.

Occasionally I have tried with American models to compose a "deadly dozen" flies for fishing in streams. Eight or nine of them have been dry flies in sizes from No. 10 down to 18 or 20, while a dozen for still-water fishing have included only 3-4 dry flies. The rest have been wet flies, such as some ample servings of Muddler Minnow, Wooly Bugger, and Bitch Creek Nymph. Nor have still-water dry flies been of negligible

size. The successful Swedish dry fly Streaking Caddis, which imitates a caddis fly and is tied by muddler techniques, has also been included in the dozen for stream fishing, in size No. 8 - besides a wasp No. 10 and a flying ant No. 12.

An exception here is to have a dry midge of size No. 18 or 20 for the golden chances that arise towards the end of autumn, when food is getting scarce in small lakes and the rainbow trout are feverishly hunting what is left - especially midges.

Only two flies have been common to both of these "dozens", apart from the above-mentioned Streaking Caddis. One is Hare's Ear, an imitation of big mayfly nymphs and hatchers as well as big caddis-fly pupae. The other is a Muddler Minnow which sometimes can be an effective lifesaver in either flowing or still waters. But I freely admit that it is difficult to limit the range of favorite flies to just a dozen when fishing in still water. There, the fish are so diverse in diet that I often think every lake deserves its own "deadly dozen".

So a recommendation is that all still-water flyfishermen, when touring several different kinds of waters, take along a field kit in their baggage - namely a reduced set of flytying tools that makes it possible to improvise imitations of those insects and other goodies which the fish prefer at the moment. A collection of ready-made flies that can fully cover all fishing opportunities in all lakes would scarcely be transportable!

Nonetheless, we shall now try to pare down the list of favorites for still water, while also identifying - as far as possible - the insects that they imitate, and which fishing tactic is suitable to them.

Choosing a fly can be difficult – sometimes very difficult indeed. But there are several reliable favorite flies that will tempt the fish in most types of still water.

Large mayflies

The largest mayfly species in Scandinavia's still waters is *Ephemera vulgata*, the "green drake". Its color, from dirty yellow to deep chocolate-brown, is darker than that of the "drake" in flowing waters, *Ephemera danica*. Yet many of the classic mayfly patterns are applicable to it. The kind found most effective by experienced flyfishermen in still waters is tied with burnt feather-wings, parachute hackle and a free rear body, on dry-fly hooks of sizes 10-12.

These imitations are used during early summer in north European waters. It generally takes a couple of days before the hatching starts to excite the fish - but then they often hunt the newly hatched mayflies with a frenzy, splashing almost violently as they rise. One can even see rainbow and brown trout jumping half a meter above the surface in attempts to snap up the flies, and their acrobatics frequently succeed.

During this period the fish are easy enough to catch, if you manage to place your fly on their beat. At the same time, a still-water flyfisherman has fine chances of hooking a real heavyweight - for the feast is shared by all the fish, big and small.

However, as a rule it does not last long. It may occur during several periods of varying intensity, depending on the weather. But the fish soon discover greater rewards in trying to snap up these mayflies before they hatch - particularly when they are just about to hatch, and are floating helplessly in the surface layer.

The mayfly nymph

This nymph can be imitated quite well with a large Gold Ribbed Hare's Ear, whose tail you may want to build with 4-5 fibers from a cock pheasant's tail feather. The result, though, has one drawback: unless greased, it does not float very long if at all.

Therefore, assuming that the same nymph is not to be used also as an imitation of large mayfly pupae (in that case without tail-strands, since the pupae lack such a tail), you can replace the nymph's front section with a more or less equally thick thorax of deer hair, and leave a little bunch of hair tips on each side while dressing it. These bunches imitate the wing rudiments of a hatching "green drake". But the most important thing with this tying method is to obtain an imitation hatcher which floats ungreased - and floats in the underside of the water surface, just like its real prototype.

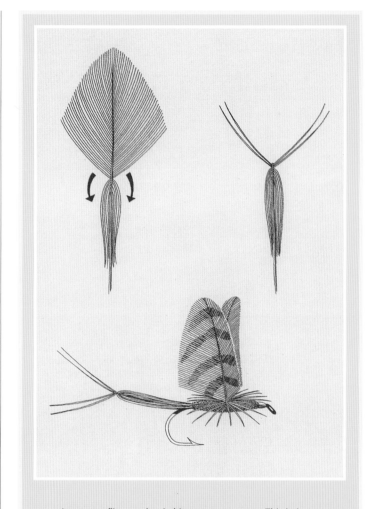

Large mayflies can be tied in numerous ways. This imitation of a "green drake" (dun), tied with parachute hackle, is quite effective – but the pattern must naturally be varied in color and size, depending on which mayflies occur locally.

GREEN DRAKE (DUN)

Hook: *dry-fly hook with downward eye No. 10-12*

Tying thread: *brown*

Tail and reversed hackle: *"wonderwing"-tied badger saddle hackle feather, with four fibers left and bent backward as tail antennae*

Front body: *medium-brown poly dubbing*

Wings: *two burnt pheasant breast feathers, 13-15 mm (0.5-0.6 in) long, tied back to back*

Hackle: *light brown cock, parachute-tied around the wing root*

Head: *black*

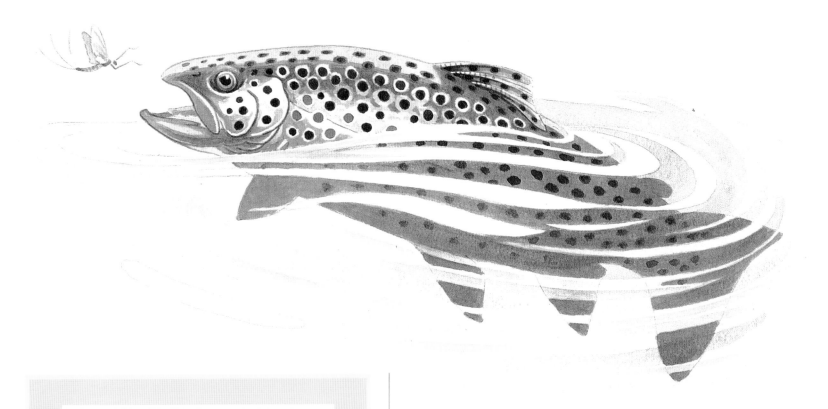

Above: The challenge may be to tempt the trout with an imitation of big mayflies.

This nymph can be fished either weighted or unweighted. If greased, it floats and provides an excellent imitation of large, hatching mayflies and caddis-fly pupae.

GOLD-RIBBED HARE'S EAR (NYMPH)

Hook: *long-shanked wet-fly hook or streamer hook No. 10-14*

Tying thread: *brown*

Tail: *a sparse bunch, 5 mm (0.2 in) long, of pheasant cock tail feather fibers - or, for small hook sizes, a little bunch of brown cock hackle fibres*

Rear body: *dubbed brown, gray, and black fur from a hare's ear, ribbed with round or oval gold tinsel*

Front body: *somewhat darker and thicker dubbing from a hare's ear, with longer hairs "pushed out" to imitate legs and wing cases*

Head: *clear varnish over the tying thread*

One seldom needs other mayfly imitations, or for that matter any special version of the "green drake" such as a spent spinner - the form which falls onto the water with outstretched wings. It does happen that the fish feed wildly on spent spinners, but even then your dun imitations can be applied with great success. A slight trick is enough to make them work wonders: jerk the line to give them a bit of life. Experience shows that the fish, however hungry for dead mayflies, will always prefer them alive if the choice exists.

STREAKING CADDIS

Hook: *dry-fly hook with downward eye No. 8-12*

Tying thread: *black or brown, extra strong*

Body: *dark-beige or olive-green poly dubbing, amply tied over the rear half of the hook shank and slightly down into the hook bend*

Wing and head: *muddler-tied with brown or grey-brown deer's hair, clipped so that the fly's underside is flat and the winglhead shape is a pointed triangle*

EUROPA 12

Hook: *dry-fly hook with downward eye No. 10-16*

Tying thread: *yellow*

Tail: *a short bunch of pheasant hen tailfeather fibers*

Body (2/3 of the hook shaft): *dubbed fur from hare's ear, or medium-grey poly yarn*

Ribbing: *yellow floss silk*

Wings: *mallard hen breast feathers, tied in sedge fashion over the body and tail*

Hackle: *brown cock*

Head: *clear varnish over the tying thread*

Large caddis flies

Imitations of caddis flies, whether the complete winged ones or the larvae and pupae, play an enormous and indeed predominant role when it comes to flyfishing in still waters. This is comparable to the significance of mayfly imitations in flowing waters, although caddis-fly imitations are responsible for much of the catch there as well.

Caddis flies are abundant in virtually all waters. There are several hundred species, ranging from very small flies that require imitations on No. 16-18 hooks to gigantic ones with a body length of 30-35 mm (1.2-1.4 in).

The best-known imitation in Europe is No. 12 in the French Europea series. Tied in various sizes on hook numbers 8-16, it imitates a wide range of caddis-fly species. For some years there has also been a Swedish pattern, now extremely popular in Scandinavia and spreading beyond Europe - the

Streaking Caddis. This is simple but ingenious: a fat banana-shaped body of poly yarn, with a muddler head which is dressed so that the deer-hair tips on the hook's upper side form the fly's wings, creating the characteristic "roof" of a caddis fly at rest.

Streaking Caddis is an unsinkable imitation, and this is important. For the fishing technique that makes it so effective is based upon adept manipulation of the line, which enables the fly to copy the slithering movement on the water surface that is typical of the big, egg-laying caddis flies and is apparently quite provocative to large rainbow and brown trout.

The most successful time for Streaking Caddis is at dusk and night - when the fisherman can no longer see the fly, but will surely hear the noise of the fish striking at it! A Streaking Caddis should then be kept moving with long, distinct pulls of 30-40 cm (1.0-1.3 ft) on the line, at intervals of 5-6

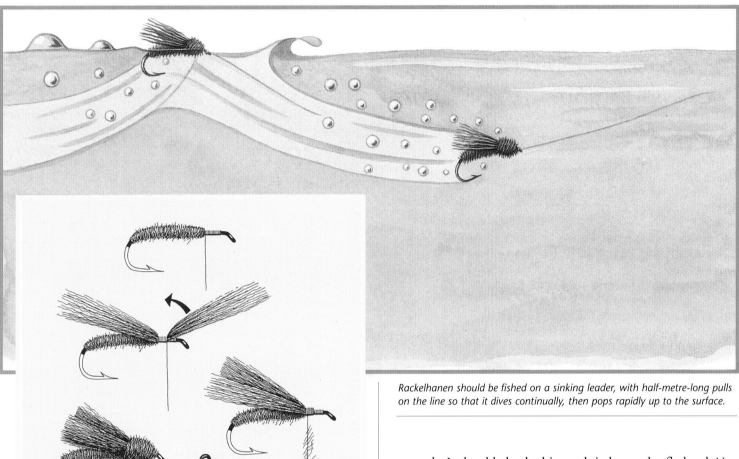

Rackelhanen should be fished on a sinking leader, with half-metre-long pulls on the line so that it dives continually, then pops rapidly up to the surface.

The original version of Rackelhanen has brown wings and body, but many variants have been created. The most popular are one with an olive-green body and beige wings, and another with black body and white wings on hook size No.16.

RACKELHANEN

Hook: *dry-fly hook with downward eye No. 10-16*

Tying thread: *brown*

Rear body: *dark-brown or cinnamon-brown thick poly dubbing, amply tied over the rear 3/4 of the hook shaft*

Wings: *dark-brown or cinnamon-brown poly dubbing, which forms a backward- and upward-pointing V over the rear body*

Head: *a ball of dark-brown or cinnamon-brown, thick poly dubbing*

seconds. It should also be big, and tied on a dry-fly hook No. 8 or 10. Yet this clever fly is equally excellent for fishing in daylight, and it has proved able to tempt even huge grayling that are otherwise unreceptive.

Medium-sized caddis flies

This group of caddis flies was once imitated almost always with Europea No. 12. But that universal fly has recently met growing competition from a new favorite, Rackelhanen. Its Swedish name refers to a hybrid of two large wild wood-hens, the black grouse and capercaillie. The fly thus named is also a kind of hybrid - it imitates both the hatching pupa and the complete winged caddis fly.

The original Rackelhanen fly was invented by the well-known Swedish flyfisherman and rod-maker Kenneth Bostrom. It was made entirely of thick dark-brown poly yarn, apart from the hook and tying thread. This material gives the fly - especially if greased - an outstanding buoyancy which is important for its fishing technique. Rackelhanen must be fished with a "wet", slowly sinking leader, and with pulls of about 15 cm (6 in) on the line, which make the fly dive and then pop up again.

Caddis-fly pupae

There are a lot of imitations of the pupae as well, and the same patterns are used in lakes as in streams. We have already mentioned one of them, Gold-Ribbed Hare's Ear, which seems to work as nicely when imitating pupae as when the fish are hunting mayfly nymphs about to hatch.

Nalle Puh from Finland, too, has a pupa version - tied in sizes from hook No. 10 to 16, with the rear body usually dirty orange or with olive-green dubbing. These imitations have rough, very shaggy bodies which, during the fishing, retain plenty of air in small glittering bubbles, thus adroitly copying the gas-filled coat of a pupa.

In the past two or three years, however, Nalle Puh has competed increasingly often with something called the Super-pupa. This is a series of six or seven patterns, in sizes from hook No. 8 to 16. They have traditional shaggy bodies of rough poly dubbing or natural underfur. The trick is their body hackle, which winds over both the rear and front of the body, and is clipped over and under the hook shaft.

The Superpupa becomes a floating pupa imitation if it is greased - otherwise it sinks slowly. Like other pupa imitations, it can be tied in a great number of color combinations. The best fishing results have been obtained with three versions: No. 16 with dark gray body and dark-blue dun body hackle, nicely imitating small caddis-fly pupae as well as all sorts of other nymphs that are eaten especially by Arctic char; No. 14 with olive rear body and a very darkbrown thorax; and No. 8 with cream-colored rear body, dark-brown thorax and light-brown body hackle. The last of these is fished primarily as a dry fly, either motionless or with short, cautious line jerks. It seldom arouses the fish in streams, but in still waters it has been a terrible killer.

Not only did the Superpupa become a new favorite - it also ushered in a whole new kind of flyfishing. That is, it turned out to be the best fly known until now for catching whitefish, usually a nerve-wracking ordeal. In many waters, whitefish are specialized to eat the drifting insects, largely caddis-fly pupae, which hover some centimeters beneath the surface. An ungreased Superpupa is cast upstream of the whitefish by 3-4 m (10-13 ft) in a stream, while in lakes it is placed 5-6 m (16-20 ft) in front of foraging schools of whitefish so that it can sink to the right depth before they see it. Moreover, it is enjoyed not only by whitefish; you will often get a "bonus" catch of sizeable trout and Arctic char.

All of this pupa fishing has been done with imitations which are presented in, or just under, the water surface. But caddis-fly pupae begin their journey to the surface from the bottom, and throughout the trip they are attacked by greedy fish. Commonly only a few percent of the pupae escape being taken and manage to hatch on the surface in order to reach their fourth and final stage. Yet these few are enough to ensure the insect family's survival.

Imitating a caddis fly that climbs out of the bottom gravel to start its adventurous voyage, though, is hardly easy. Indeed, it may appear hopeless to make a deep-sinking imitation work naturally. This has been done, but mainly in flowing water and by using Frank Sawyer's awfully ingenious Killer Bug. In lakes we should stick to the surface layer, where the fish also certainly come, sooner or later, in their quest for rapidly rising pupae.

Even when fishing in still water, one should act cautiously and try to keep a low profile.

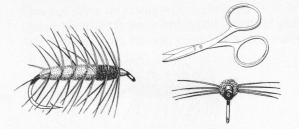

The Superpupa is a terrific pupa imitation which, besides the original (below), also comes in variants: one with an olive-green rear body on hook No. 12-14 and, for Arctic char, one with a dark-grey rear body on hook No. 16.

SUPERPUPA

Hook: dry-fly hook with downward eye No. 8-16

Tying thread: same color as the rear body

Rear body: cream-coloured, light or dark olive, or darkgrey poly dubbing, amply tied over 2/3 of the hook shank

Front body: dark-brown or black poly dubbing

Body hackle: cock hackle over both the front and rear body, light brown (if the rear body is cream-colored) or blue dun, or (if the rear body is dark grey) dark blue dun. The hackle is clipped down over and under the hook shank.

Head: clear varnish over the tying thread

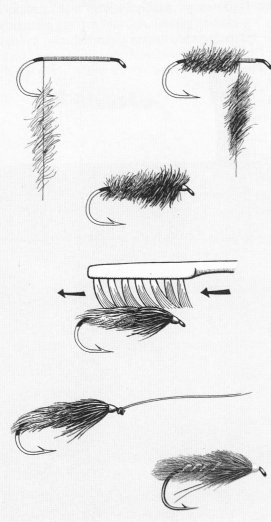

NALLE PUH (PUPA)

Hook: wet-fly hook No. 10-16

Tying thread: beige, brorwn or olive green (according to the rear body color)

Rear body: beige, dark orange or olive green, synthetic dubbing of rough, glittering materials. The rear body is tied amply, then "combed " so that it can retain tiny air bubbles (the above illustration shows, too, a variant with a silver-ribbed rear body).

Front body: thick, ample dubbing from hare's ear with pushed-out hairs

Head: clear varnish over the tying thread

KILLER BUG

Hook: wet-fly hook No. 8-14 Tying thread and weighting thin red copper wire

Body: three layers of copper wire, under an ample body of red, brown, and grey wool yarn (Chadwick No. 477)

Head: three or four turns of copper wire

Killer Bug was invented by the well known English fly-fisherman Frank Sawyer. This fly sinks fast and can there-fore be made to imitate a caddis-fly pupa climbing from the boffom toward the surface. The copper wire is attached where the hook bend begins, then wound tight-ly forward to just behind the hook eye, and finally wound backward. When it reaches the hook bend, it is used to attach the Chadwickyarn, then wound forward again to just behind the hook eye. Lastly the yarn is wound for-ward and fastened with the copper wire.

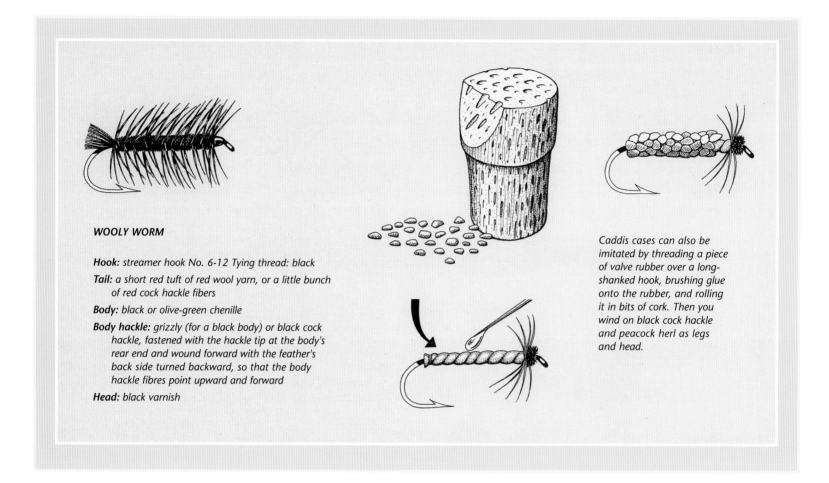

WOOLY WORM

Hook: *streamer hook No. 6-12 Tying thread: black*

Tail: *a short red tuft of red wool yarn, or a little bunch of red cock hackle fibers*

Body: *black or olive-green chenille*

Body hackle: *grizzly (for a black body) or black cock hackle, fastened with the hackle tip at the body's rear end and wound forward with the feather's back side turned backward, so that the body hackle fibres point upward and forward*

Head: *black varnish*

Caddis cases can also be imitated by threading a piece of valve rubber over a long-shanked hook, brushing glue onto the rubber, and rolling it in bits of cork. Then you wind on black cock hackle and peacock herl as legs and head.

Caddis cases

Many caddis flies are at the larval stage of case-builders, which put together a tube-shaped dwelling that covers and protects their rear bodies and part of their front bodies. When they move - slowly and clumsily, since they drag the case with them - you can see their heads and legs projecting from the case's front end.

Some birds strip caddis cases before eating them. Fish cannot do this, but swallow them whole, and this unavoidable "house consumption" explains all the rubbish - pine needles, wood bits, grains of gravel - which is often found in the otherwise empty stomachs of rainbow and brown trout.

Caddis-fly larvae are easy to imitate. The case-building larvae use whatever materials are nearest, and these are often pieces of vegetation, which enable us to imitate the worms with a weighted version of an American favorite, Wooly

Worm. This fly has the right caseworm profile, being made of chenille - the best body material and available in numerous colors (mainly dark olive and black). A weighted Wooly Worm can and should be fished deep, with matchstick-long jerks of the line.

In certain lakes and streams, however, caddis-fly larvae choose a different building material: sand and gravel, which make them harder to copy. An old French method was to thread about 2 cm (0.8 in) of bicycle-tire valve rubber over a long-shafted hook, brush the valve with glue, and roll it in gravel. It is difficult to cast, but its lumpiness can be avoided by imitating the gravel as well - namely with bits of cork, shaved off a wine cork with a rough file! The larva's head and legs on such a valve-rubber fly can be imitated with, for example, a "head" of wound peacock herl, or one or two turns of black cock hackle.

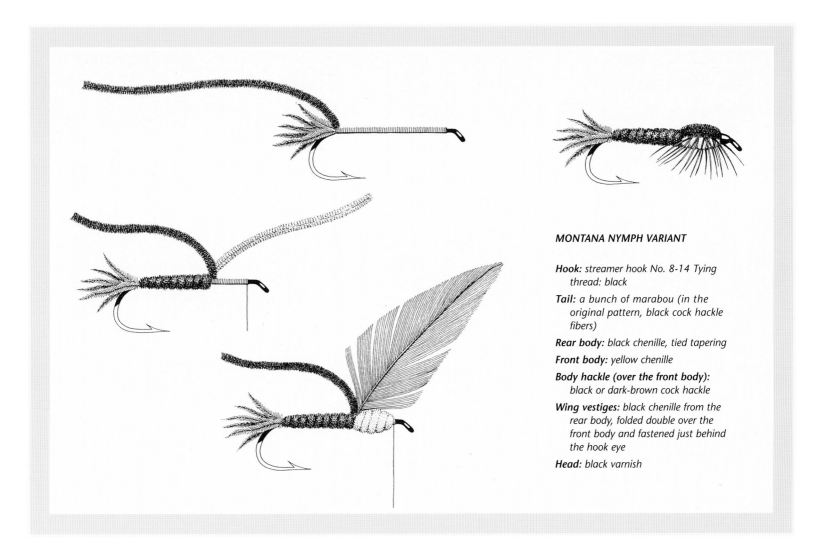

MONTANA NYMPH VARIANT

Hook: *streamer hook No. 8-14 Tying thread: black*

Tail: *a bunch of marabou (in the original pattern, black cock hackle fibers)*

Rear body: *black chenille, tied tapering*

Front body: *yellow chenille*

Body hackle (over the front body): *black or dark-brown cock hackle*

Wing vestiges: *black chenille from the rear body, folded double over the front body and fastened just behind the hook eye*

Head: *black varnish*

Damselflies

This is another interesting family of "flyfishing insects". They play little role in flowing waters, but are extremely important - almost always as nymphs - for fishing in still waters. One should, though, take along one or two good representatives of the few exceptions, meaning imitations of complete winged damselflies.

For it happens that one sees fine rainbow trout which have specialized on, and developed a fine hunting technique for, "dry" damselflies. The fact is that damselflies like to sit on leaves, for example of water-lilies. They sit along the leaf edges with their heads bent out towards open water. Since they can see well and react very fast, the trout have to surprise them, from behind if possible. The fish does so by taking aim, flipping itself over the leaf with its mouth open,

and catching the damselfly on the way back into the water on the other side.

But the flyfisherman seldom gets such a chance, as the main role is played by damselfly nymphs. These abound almost everywhere in Scandinavian still waters, except in the mountains - and the fish adore them. While they are not hard to imitate, you will have much more success with patterns that are impressions rather than imitations. The best by far is a Montana Nymph Variant, on which the oarlike gills are copied by a 5-mm long tuss of marabou herl, which makes the nymph wave its tail realistically in the water. This fly is tied in two sizes, on streamer hooks Nos. 10 and 12, both weighted and unweighted. The fly is kept moving with short, distinct jerks or twists of the fly line, because a damselfly nymph moves jerkily.

Ants

Ants, too, play an extensive role in still-water fishing, particularly in the thousands of small lakes in forest regions. Some years ago, a Scandinavian scientist made a study of the food habits of implanted rainbow, brown, and brook trout. It was found that no other food dominated their menu so heavily as did ants during the month of August. This applied to all of the lakes investigated, and the proportion of ants in the fish's food reached 80 percent.

The explanation is that flying ants swarm intensively at close intervals in late summer. They "rain" down on lakes by the billions - up to several hundred per square meter of water surface - and attract all fish to the surface.

At the beginning of an ant swarming, when the ants fall rather sparsely, the fish are easy to catch, being equally eager and unafraid, so that the competition for tit-bits of food is strong. But just a few minutes later, it can be almost impossible to hook a single fish, even though they rise madly. The real ants are then too numerous, and a fish is extremely unlikely to take an imitation ant by mistake.

But towards the end of the swarming, ants fall less densely again and the flyfisherman has his chance. Fish in lakes that are blessed with such swarmings become obsessed with ants, so for a long time - often several weeks - imitation ants remain by far the best flies to use, even on occasions when there are no ants or any other fish food on the surface.

Ant imitations are easy to tie. Two examples may be mentioned. One consists of a couple of "balls" of fine black poly dubbing, separated by a sparse black cock hackle. The wings are not important, but sometimes they are added, made of light-gray cock hackle tips and tied in a V shape between the poly balls.

McMurray Ant is another effective imitation of ants. Thefly has superb catching ability, but can be hard to tie – or rather, manufacture – and it seldom lastsfor more than one strike. It is made by sandpapering balsa balls and joining them with a stump of epoxy-glued whole nylon line. The balls are varnished and tied onto the hook shaft. Finally the hackle, of black or brown cock hackle, is wound on and fastened with the tying thread.

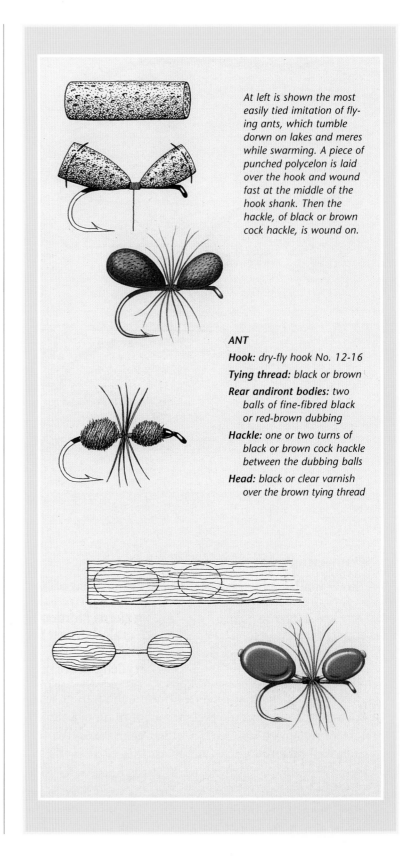

At left is shown the most easily tied imitation of flying ants, which tumble dorwn on lakes and meres while swarming. A piece of punched polycelon is laid over the hook and wound fast at the middle of the hook shank. Then the hackle, of black or brown cock hackle, is wound on.

ANT

Hook: dry-fly hook No. 12-16

Tying thread: black or brown

Rear andiront bodies: two balls of fine-fibred black or red-brown dubbing

Hackle: one or two turns of black or brown cock hackle between the dubbing balls

Head: black or clear varnish over the brown tying thread

A flyfisherman's shadow plays on a cliff alongside a lake. During the evenings and mornings, the fish are often extremely active.

Wasps

Besides flying ants, a great many other land insects become fish food now and then: crane-flies, sloebugs, bumblebees, wasps, peppered moth larvae, grasshoppers, and all sorts of small flies, beetles and so on.

The most important of these are definitely wasps, which may tumble down in such numbers during the summer and early autumn that they make the fish rise eagerly. A wasp rain can result, for example, from a thunderstorm or a frosty night that renders the wasps almost unable to fly.

It is frequently very hard to see whether wasps are the reason why fish are rising. Wasps themselves are quite difficult to see when they have fallen onto the water. Being heavy insects, they lie deep in the surface layer and may well be noticed only if you look straight down at them. But the fish can indicate what is going on by their powerful, gurgling whirls, like the wake of a energetic paddle.

Wasps are imitated in various ways - for instance, similarly to the simple ants made of poly dubbing, but alternating the black poly with dark orange in order to copy the characteristic stripes on a wasp's rear body. Another method resembles the McMurray Ant, using varnished balsa. Or a muddler technique is applicable, ideally with reindeer hair, which is easy to colour black and dark orange.

The popularity of wasps is greatest among rainbow trout. An insect that can evoke the same response is the sloebug, although this smelly creature is by no means as plentiful, and thus not so worth trying to imitate.

Snails

The insects discussed above are basically worldwide - their species may differ from place to place, but the families they represent are found everywhere and the behaviour of fish in regard to eating them is surprisingly universal.

Top right: This wasp imitation can, of course, also be given wings, such as light-grey hackle tips that are tied on between the rear and front bodies. But ant- and wasp-eating fish will take the wingless variety just as readily.

Bottom right: Wasp imitations can also be made in the same way as McMurray Ant – with balsa balls that are sandpapered smooth and varnished in "wasp colours". The hook shank is then glued into a cutout groove. Finally the hackle, of dark-brown or black cock hackle feather, is wound on.

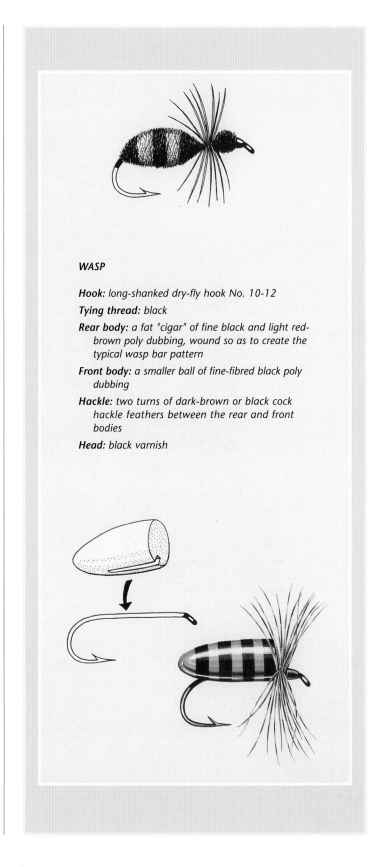

WASP

Hook: *long-shanked dry-fly hook No. 10-12*

Tying thread: *black*

Rear body: *a fat "cigar" of fine black and light red-brown poly dubbing, wound so as to create the typical wasp bar pattern*

Front body: *a smaller ball of fine-fibred black poly dubbing*

Hackle: *two turns of dark-brown or black cock hackle feathers between the rear and front bodies*

Head: *black varnish*

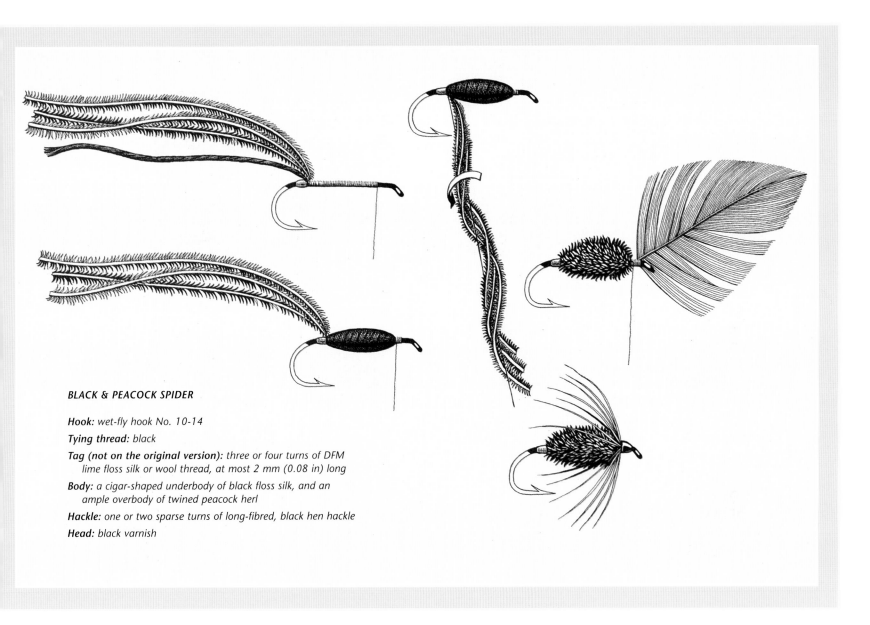

BLACK & PEACOCK SPIDER

Hook: *wet-fly hook No. 10-14*

Tying thread: *black*

Tag (not on the original version): *three or four turns of DFM lime floss silk or wool thread, at most 2 mm (0.08 in) long*

Body: *a cigar-shaped underbody of black floss silk, and an ample overbody of twined peacock herl*

Hackle: *one or two sparse turns of long-fibred, black hen hackle*

Head: *black varnish*

One kind of fish food that was described in a pioneering book, *Still-Water Flyfishing* by Tom Ivens, published thirty years ago, was the relatively unknown group of "pulmonate" (lung-bearing) snails which, during the summer, migrate in great numbers through lakes by drifting with the wind and waves.

It was soon discovered that such snails occur abundantly also outside England - in meres and ponds as well as lakes - and that they are just as appealing to fish there as in the British freshwater reservoirs. In his book, Tom Ivens recom-mends an imitation named Black & Peacock Spider, whose greatest success occurred during August and September.

Ivens' fly does not closely resemble the snail – or slug which it is supposed to imitate, but it is extraordinarily effective if fished very slowly in, or just under, the water surface. That the fish, whether rainbow or brown trout, seem to believe it really is a snail, has been well-proved by the present author. Many of the fish in such catches have turned out to be stuffed with pulmonate snails, and nothing else.

Waterboatmen

Yet another insect that fish in still waters love to gobble is the waterboatman - in Scandinavia and Great Britain alike, as well as in the United States, New Zealand, and several other countries with freshwater salmonoids.

The most common imitation of waterboatmen is British in origin. But success does not always follow with this fly on the leader. For these insects do not occur in all lakes, and only on special occasions do the fish concentrate upon eating that particular family. However, such occasions are memorable indeed, arising mainly when the waterboatmen are swarming. They normally live underwater, but have to come up at regular intervals to renew their air supply, and then they make miniature "wakes" on the surface. When swarming, they fold out the wings hidden under their shoulder-scales, and ascend from the water like Polaris missiles, heading for dry land in order to mate.

After mating, they return in thousands to resume life in the water, and may then form a "rain" of water boatmen. This recalls a hailstorm, as insects fall all over the surface with short, sharp plopping sounds - and the fish react with the same enthusiasm as when ants are swarming. But you have to be lucky to experience it.

Lures

Lures are often large and unlike any known insects. In flowing waters they offer little to the flyfisherman, but they can be exceedingly effective in still waters. When fishing the latter, therefore, you should always take along at least three such odd patterns of different sizes: a Wooly Bugger, a Bitch Creek Nymph - both of them heavily weighted - and a Muddler Minnow, which is the one that can also sometimes give good results in flowing water as well.

Wooly Bugger, which has a fine British counterpart named Dog Nobbler, is tied on a streamer hook No. 8, 10 or 12. The other two patterns call for streamer hook No. 8 and 10. Nobody knows what a Wooly Bugger or Dog Nobbler is supposed to represent, but perhaps the fish take them for leeches. Anyhow they are frequently murderous, especially when fishing for rainbow trout.

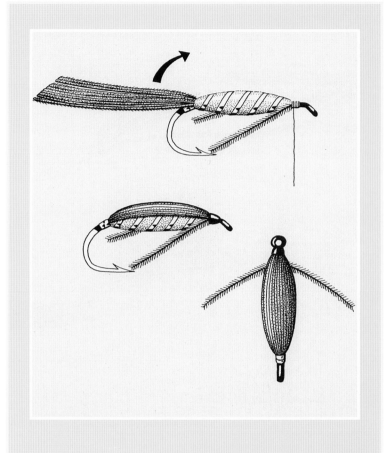

CORIXA

Hook: *wet-fly hook No. 10-14*
Tying thread: *brown*
Body: *amply tied of white floss silk, ribbed with round or oval silver tinsel*
Wing cases: *a bunch of pheasant cock tail feather fibres, tied in at the hook bend, folded forward and fastened at the head*
Legs: *thin peacock herl, one on each side of the body*
Head: *clear varnish over the tying thread*

Right: When fishing in lakes, a long rod and light line are preferable.

Flyfishing in Streams

A waterway's character and geographical location are decisive for the kind of salmonoid fish to be found there. Of course, it has always been difficult for human beings to accept that all fish - especially those in fresh waters - have a limited natural distribution. When we learned the rather simple craft of squeezing eggs from fish and raising trout or salmon fry, we immediately started spreading them into waters where they had not existed. If they were able to spawn and get enough food, they accept ed the new environment.

This is why salmonoids occur at all in the Southern Hemisphere - for instance in New Zealand, Tasmania and Australia as well as in South America, where some of the world's best trout fishing is now found. These places have never possessed natural stocks of salmonoids, which origin ally were confined to our Northern Hemisphere.

The English, in particular, have made a great and laud able effort to implant trout almost everywhere in their former colonies. Residents who had long been away from "good old England" needed at least a few trout to swing their rods at! But the introduction of trout to new waters has not been entirely a positive trend. In many places the new species have prospered enough to completely eradicate the original ones. As a result, several excellent and rare fish species have been lost to posterity. Good examples are the numerous subspecies of the cutthroat trout (*Salmo clarki*), which spread over North America by adapting themselves to the existing water system and its environment.

The massive stocking of salmon and trout from artificial hatcheries has also "diluted" the valuable gene pool of the few surviving wild fish, an inheritance which has taken millennia of adaptation to evolve and which cannot be recreated once it is gone. Often we know nothing about the gene pool of cultured fish, which are commonly degenerated and domesticated after having lived in confinement for generations. Incurable damage has been caused by the uncritical stocking of such unknown material through the years.

The rainbow trout (*Salmo gairdneri)* has thus come to inhabit most of the world, where conditions are suitable for it. But even the European brown trout (*Salmo trutta*) has crossed the seven seas and can now be found in America as well as Australia. The grayling (*Thymallus thymallus*), whose farming is a little more complicated and therefore of smaller commercial value, has not travelled so widely, and exists mainly in the places where nature originally put it.

Holding places

All of the above-mentioned salmonoids live more or less permanently in the same waterways. Some fish may occasionally make visits to a nearby lake, but they are otherwise bound to the stream where they hunt and reproduce. When we fish for them, we must therefore remember that they have a constant need of cover and of food. So we have to look for them where they can fulfill both of these requirements.

This sounds easy in theory, but is harder in practice, due to the great differences between waterways. Each has its own character, and not until we get to know it can we "read" the water and find the fish. Not only that - there are also significant differences between the fish species. Moreover, the fish seldom occur at the same places in summer as in winter. Consequently, locating them in a new and unfamiliar body of water may strike us as a daunting task.

It isn't, though: with a little common sense, as well as some knowledge of fish and their living habits, we can go a long way. To begin with, there is a vast distinction between a slow chalk stream and a rushing river. For example, the current lee is very important to the fish in a river, but not in a chalk stream. Thus it is easier to find the fish in a fast current, where the holding places are clearly visible in its lee. Such places can hardly be noticed in a chalk stream, whose fish occur virtually everywhere - and may hold in the most surprising spots - so that we have to approach the water with extreme caution.

In the Alps of Central Europe, waterways have long been divided into a trout region and a grayling region. In the former, far up in the mountains where the brooks crash down the cliffs, the red-spotted brown trout is the sole ruler of the cold, rushing melt-water. Farther down as the slopes flatten out, we enter the region dominated by grayling - even though trout can sometimes be caught there as well.

This division is not exactly applicable to other parts of the world, but it tells a little about the fish and their demands on the environment. While brown trout can certainly be discovered in the quietest waterways, grayling never occur up in the mountains.

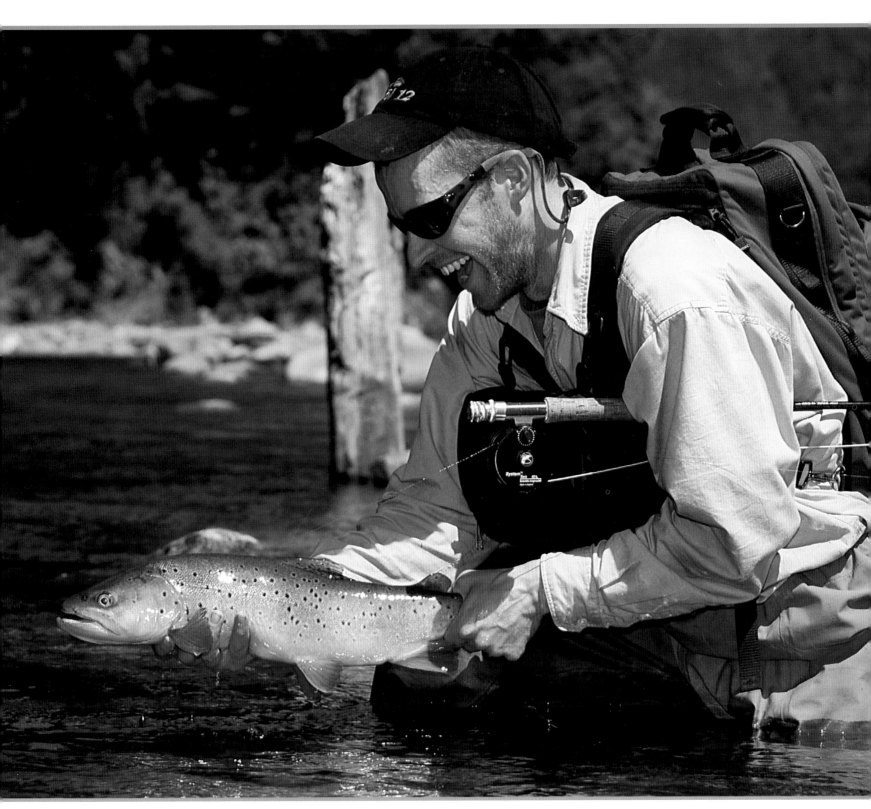

Small flowing waters can offer real surprises and hold much bigger fish than is commonly believed.
Trout exist all over the world and are a classic catch for the flyfisherman in flowing water.

The same stretch of flowing water is shown here from above and in cross-section. Illustrated in the inset above are some typical holding places: *(A)* before or alongside stones and boulders, *(B)* just behind or under rich water vegetation that provides shade and protection, *(C)* under the protective hanging parts of trees, shore banks, and large roots. Other common places where fish often hold are, in particular, the necks of rapids and the deep calm water which follows a rapid or a stretch of current.

As was noted earlier, grayling often form small shoals at calm places in a waterway. By contrast, trout are definite loners and do not tolerate other fish in their territory. They also want "a roof over their heads" - being able to hold under a precipice, bank hollow, or overhanging tree. Thus, they are closely tied to shores or at least to fixed structures; yet grayling prefer to stay near the bottom in deep water. Further, whereas grayling are mainly active by day, trout tend to be nocturnal, and big ones are notably shy during the daytime, when they stay well hidden in their holding places. At night they may hunt in amazingly shallow water, where they are also easy to frighten!

An intermediate case is the rainbow trout: seldom clearly nocturnal, but not a shoal fish either. The rarer brook trout prefers a solitary life in deep water, but is normally the greediest of all trout species - a characteristic which it shares with the cutthroat trout, mentioned above, so that both of them are vulnerable to overfishing. In other words, they cannot take the same fishing pressure as does the brown trout, which is shy and soon learns to avoid the fisherman's bait.

These are, to be sure, generalizations that must be adjusted to suit the given fishing waters. But all fish have in common the fact that their holding places differ between summer and winter. In summer, when the water is warm, they gladly move to a stream whose water contains more oxygen. In winter the opposite is true, since their metabolism is slower in the cold water. Then they leave the fast streams and gather in calm places, where they can stand in the current lee to save energy.

It is impossible to specify all the types of holding places in a small waterway, so only the real "classics" will be described here. Among them is the calm water in a pool, below a rapid or a stretch of current. The fish stay in the pool's deep, quiet water and benefit from the food that is brought continually by the current. Usually the fish can be found at the deep upstream end during the hours of light. As darkness falls, the fish often retreat to feed in the shallow water at the pool's lower end, where the current is stronger.

The necks of rapids, with deep and relatively calm water just above a waterfall or rapid, are further good holding places. So is the area where water from a fall pours down into a pool, or even simply a pocket of deep water. Frequently the fish stand all the way into the spray! And large stones or cliffs in the main stream are invariably potential holding places, worth being fished carefully. The fish seldom stand behind stones - where the water tends to be too rough - but generally stay in front or along the sides. There and at the front, a current lee provides the fish with a good vantage point to watch for food brought by the current.

In calm waters, the fish are more bound to the deep channels, especially at the bends where the current has dug into the banks and often hollowed them out. Brown trout are notable lovers of such dug-out banks. Fish also like to linger near the channels that are formed by areas of vegetation. Here the current collects drifting insects and crustaceans, which thus become easy prey.

Trees that have fallen into a stream offer the fish both cover and current lee. A lot of fish may also be found in large pools with quiet backwaters. Except during the cold season, however, fish seldom hold in the backwater itself, but frequently stay just where the current enters or leaves the pool. The backwater exhibits instead, for example, pike and perch. Unlike the salmonoids, these fish do not really belong there - they merely look for places where the current is weakest.

As a whole, the fish are more shy and cautious in small waterways than in big ones. The more water runs over and around the fish, the more secure they feel. In a small stream, therefore, we must be very careful when getting close to the water and the fish. It is best to keep a low profile, moving slowly and wearing clothes that merge into the surroundings as much as possible.

Then the point of readiness has come to start fishing, which can be quite exciting in brooks and streams. Everything happens at close range, making it essential to have full control over both flies and fish. At the same time, small waterways are good schools for the inexperienced flyfisherman, who can learn many things about the fish there and can later apply the lessons to larger, more limitless waterways.

Fish are frequently difficult to see in flowing water, but they may be detectable if you approach the water very carefully.

Types of rise

One very important thing a flyfisherman should be able to do is read different "rise forms". When the fish takes an insect at or near the water surface, it leaves rings or ripples on the surface. These serve to show the fisherman what sort of insect, and in which stage, the fish takes. On this basis the fly is chosen to catch the fish with.

The rise form is the visible sign of the fish's activity, and it can have quite diverse appearances - depending on the insect species, the fish's size and the water movement. In any case, the rise itself is the essence of flyfishing: it means direct eye contact with a hunting fish. Hardly any other sight can be so stimulating, or indeed so frustrating if you fail to catch the fish, which either flees in fright or goes on rising nonchalantly.

It has to be emphasized firstly that a flyfisherman should always wear Polaroid glasses. They not only protect the eyes from a wildly moving fly, but also filter out many of the irritating reflections that prevent you from seeing into the water. Hence they are at least as important as the rod, reel, line and fly - in fact more important, as they provide the best possibility of watching the fish under the surface even if no activity appears on the surface.

If we look farthest down into the water, a glimpse of the fish's side as it turns in the current is often all we see of it. Yet this captivating "wink under water", in the words of Skues, indicates that a fish is making a quick detour in its hunt for nymphs or other prey - a fish, therefore, which can be caught.

"Tailing": the fish eats on the bottom and shows only its tail above the water surface.

Above: "Head and tail" means that the fish takes nymphs and pupae just in or under the surface layer. First you see the head, then the back fin, and finally the tail fin over the water. However, big brown trout and steelheads often display only their backs.

Below: When a fish takes, for example, nymphs just under the surface, the water over the fish moves up and forms "bulges" on the surface. In this form of rise, you very seldom see part of the fish above the surface.

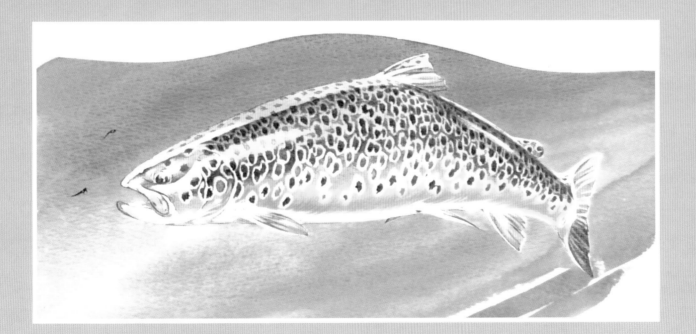

Above: When trout, and other fish in running waters, rise to take an insect that drifts on the surface, they fall back with the current. Thus you see the fish rise downstream of the holding place. To give the fish time to climb to the surface, you must therefore lay out the fly a good way upstream of the assumed holding place. Keep in mind, too, that deep fish need more time to rise than do fish near the surface.

Right: If it is impossible to figure out what the fish presently taking, trial-and-error is often necessary Experienced fishermen know that a lot of flies may have to be tried in a day before finding the "right" one for wary trout

When the water is relatively low, a phenomenon called "tailing" can be observed. In this rise form, the fish almost stands on its head in the vegetation to shake loose insects and crustaceans. It will then stick the tip of its tail out of the water, a characteristic sign. Now and then it moves downstream to pick up the creatures shaken loose, but it rapidly returns.

If the fish is hunting higher up in the water, you can frequently see it flickering in the light or lifting the water. As a result, swells are formed in the surface, leading us to speak of "bulging fish".

Commonly the fish proceeds to take the nymphs and pupae that are hanging motionless in the surface film before hatching. You see the fish "head and tail" - as first the head, then the back, and finally the tail emerge from the water, like a porpoise rolling at the surface. Here we also use the phrase "porpoise rise". When this is witnessed, you know that your leader should still be carrying a nymph, not a dry fly.

A fish takes sizeable prey such as small fish by using its jaws, but it consumes insects and other small animals by sucking them into its mouth, out of the current that flows constantly over its gills. The mouth and gill covers create a pressure drop that sucks the water in; then the mouth closes and the water is pushed back through the gill openings. Any food in the water is sieved out by the gill rakers and is swallowed.

Surface rising

When taking an insect at the surface, a fish usually sucks in some air as well. The air subsequently forms small bubbles on the surface, giving a sure sign that the fish took a winged insect at the surface - in other words, not a nymph or pupa just under it. If so, there can be no doubt that the time has come for a dry fly!

Exactly what happens on the water can be seen much more easily with a pair of binoculars. Moreover, it is always worth carefully studying what the current brings along. By combining the two sources of information, you are as wellprepared as possible, and can really pick out your fish.

We say that a fish "rises" when it takes insects on the surface. The resultant ripples, which spread downstream with the current, were once named "tell-tale rings" by an Englishman. But such rings can look very differently: they may be big or little, violent or controlled. At the violent end of the spectrum, we have fish that are in a hurry to take insects. These may be newly hatched duns, which can lift from the water at any moment and thus evade the fish. Or they may be egg-laying caddis flies that flutter over the surface, or large grasshoppers that are eager to reach dry land. All of them stimulate energetic rises, with big rings and loud splashing.

The same can happen when a fish takes small insects in a strong current, where it must act fast. It may also be a little fish that has difficulty in sucking up insects. Sometimes you then find it jumping out of the water to take the insects on the way down, so that you have to wait a bit for the counterstrike! Conversely, we often encounter very big fish which make no noise, but only leave tiny ripples on the surface, leading us to speak of "sipping" fish or a "sip rise". This latter phenomenon is typical when many small insects are hatching simultaneously on a calm surface. There is plenty of food even for a big fish, which otherwise might not be interested in small prey. It hovers just under the surface to suck in the insects at a leisurely and rather cautious pace. Such hatchings occur among

A sip rise is the commonest form of rise, producing only rings on the water surface. The rings are deceptive as their size gives no clue to the fish's weight.

the Caenis mayflies, and among the small reed knots that cover the surface at times like a carpet - or what the English call a "blanket hatch".

On very quiet stretches of current, you may meet "cruiser" fish that methodically patrol their territories to find insects on the surface. Identical behaviour is common in lakes - and there, too, it is necessary to foresee the spot at which the fish will rise the next time. Then you lay out your dry fly and wait with mounting excitement. Normally, though, a fish rises at a particular place in the waterway, giving you a natural target. Otherwise the dry fly cannot be positioned properly - that is, far enough in front of the fish, which must have time to rise to it.

A fish rises to the surface by angling its breast fins so that the current presses it upward. After taking an insect, it turns the fins downward and swims back to the bottom, assisted by a stroke of its tail. Thus, while climbing to the surface, it drops back with the current. So you see it rise a ways down stream from its holding place. And this means you should lay out your dry fly a good distance farther upstream than you per-

haps thought necessary at first, or else the fish simply won't have time to rise for it!

As a rule the fish rises from the bottom, but it may let itself come up with the current to just under the surface if there are enough insects, and if the current is not too strong. Trout do so often, whereas grayling always stay on the bottom.

In this connection you should remember that, the deeper a fish is holding, the longer time it needs to rise to the surface. Consequently the fly must be served farther upstream of the rise rings. Moreover, the fish will only rise to the insects within a narrow region, the "feeding lane", which is directly above it. Insects and flies that drift towards it out side this region are ignored. The fish does have a wide "window" and can easily see them approaching from the side, yet it will not touch them. Too much energy would be required to move sideways in a strong current, and the fish may also find it difficult to judge the distance and speed to such food. It therefore keeps its breast fins still, and takes only what passes right over its head.

A splash rise occurs when the fish rapidly chase insects that are lifting from the surface or fluttering just above it. A spray rise may occur even when the fish hunts under the surface, if it suddenly swerves at high speed to swim in another direction.

Techniques and methods
Downstream wet-fly fishing

Naturally we begin with the most classic of flyfishing's many methods. The first true flies - long before dry ones appeared - were wet flies, and they were fished downstream. This approach involves simply laying a cast across, or obliquely down, the stream toward the opposite bank. As the current takes the line, the fly follows a curve in towards your own bank. You then take a step or two downstream and repeat the procedure Thus you work your way down through the most promising stretches of water

Here is a perfect method for the beginner. For if the cast is not laid out well, the current immediately stretches the line and leader again. Besides, many fish get hooked of their own accord during downstream wet-fly fishing. So the method can hardly be more elementary - and still it is capable of refinements that make it amazingly effective in the right hands.

When a fly line is laid straight across the current, it will be pulled downstream in a wide curve. If the current is strong, the pull is so violent that the fly travels across the surface. This is not attractive to fish, and you must compensate for the current's effect by mending the line. The technique is to lift the line from the water and to shift it upstream, reducing pressure on the current. You may have to do so several times as the fly swings through the current.

Until now, we have been describing the classic "wet-fly swing", which is as effective for trout and grayling as it is for salmon and for sea trout. The only difference is that, in streams, we try to imitate the fish's food with our flies. Depending on the current speed, the line can be mended either upstream - if a fast current threatens to tear the fly out of the water - or else downstream. The latter applies if the fly happens to drift into calm water, where it will stop and sink rather lifelessly. This is avoided by mending the line downstream so that the current can take the line and fly again. You are then helping the current instead of fighting it.

Thus, when fishing in streams, mending the line is as important as making fine, exact casts. If you can't mend the line, you can't fish effectively either!

Fishing wet flies downstream is the oldest and commonest method. The line is cast across the current, or obliquely downstream, and thefly follows the flow freely until it drifts into a soft bend at your own bank Often the fish takes just as the outward fishing is ending. Also illustrated here is the fly's drift when mending.

BUTCHER

Tying thread: black
Tail: red feather fibres
Body: flat silver tinsel
Ribbing: oval silver tinsel
Wings: blue mallard wing feather
Hackle: black hen feather fibres
Head: black

TEAL & RED

Tying thread: black
Tail: golden pheasant tippets
Body: bright red wool
Ribbing: thin oval silver tinsel
Wings: teal flank feather
Hackle: brown hen feather fibres
Head: black

MARCH BROWN

Tying thread: black
Tail: brown-speckled partridge
feather fibres
Body: grey dubbed hare's fur
Ribbing: gold wire
Wings: pheasant hen wing feathers
Hackle: brown-speckled partridge
feather fibres
Head: black

This hairwinged wet fly – with dubbed wool body, hen hackle, squirrel-tail hair wing and black head – displays no special pattern but is a type of fly that has become increasingly common recently. The USA in particular has a tradition of tying soft-hackled wetflies with hair wings. Even in many of the classic wet flies, it can help to replace the feather wings with thin hair wings, which last longer and make thefly at least as attractive to the fish.

Small flies imitate small insects, which obviously lack enough strength to fight a fast current, and will therefore drift away rather lifelessly. But big flies imitate big insects or even fish fry, which can easily travel against the current. Consequently, small flies (size 12-14) should be fished with no rod movement, whereas larger flies (size 8-10) should be given extra life with the rod tip.

Many of the classic wet flies that are fished downstream were originally imitations of drowned or drowning mayflies. Examples are March Brown and Blue Dun, which should thus be fished by "dead drift" - with no rod movement. But it is more sensible to invest in fly patterns that represent fish fry to a greater extent. These are illustrated by Alexandra, Bloody Butcher and Freeman's Fancy, all with bodies of silver or gold tinsel. A downstream wet fly can be made more functional by replacing the original feather-wing with a more mobile and durable hairwing.

This kind of fishing is often regarded with some disdain as a sort of "fishing machine", covering the waterway mechanically and without any real enjoyment. That may at times be so, but never need be. It is up to the fisherman whether the fishing is to be inspired or routine. Those with insight do not fish through the stream inch by inch, but concentrate on the spots or holding places which look most promising - or on fish that reveal themselves in various ways.

If you have noticed a fish or know a good holding place, here is a useful trick. Lay your fly a fair distance upstream of the fish or holding place, with a slack line. This gives the fly time to sink a little, before the current stretches out the line and leader. When the line tightens, the fly moves up in the water and swings out towards midstream. Often the strike comes just then, as though you were pressing a button - so effective is the trick if done right. The best flies to use are wet ones with a silver or gold body and a thin hairwing. The leader must be thin, of 0.18 mm (.007 in), so that the fly can sink and move freely in the current.

When fishing out, you should make sure that the fly always fishes at the proper speed. If it starts to drag in the surface, decrease the force on it by lowering the rod tip; and if necessary, mend the line upstream. But if the fly drifts into calm water, raise the rod tip; and if this is not enough, mend the line downstream. Eventually the fly will arrive at your own bank, or downstream of you. Then you can begin a new cast.

If the water is deep and being fished from a bank, it should be fished thoroughly before taking in the line for a new cast. This can be done by pulling the line in small jerks with your left hand. Sometimes surprising results are achieved by taking in the line a little faster. A fish may rush in to snap up the fly and disappear!

On a taut line with a wet fly downstream, many fish are hooked in the actual strike. They take the fly and travel with the current, but soon realize their error. The fly does not "taste" right and they reject it. Then the strike must be quick - though not violent. It should be a controlled tightening of the line, rather than a literal striking action.

Frequently the fish can be seen taking the fly in a swirl just under the surface, whereupon you must immediately tighten the line. At other times you can only feel, or see, a gentle tug on the line - so you have to react even faster. There is always more time to spare if you see the fish take than if you simply feel it. Keep your eyes open in order to hook the fish solidly!

Upstream wet-fly fishing

Here is another of the classic methods in flyfishing. It has a lasting association with the Scotsman Stewart and his now legendary "spider" flies. Stewart fished along streams in the Scottish highlands, where the insect life was poor but sudden floods, or spates, were frequent after rainstorms. Thus the fish were seldom large and, though always hungry, they were shy and easily frightened in these small waterways.

As a professional fisherman who lived on his catches, Stewart recognized that downstream wet-fly fishing would not do under such conditions. He began to fish with wet flies in the opposite direction, and tied them so that they were specially adapted to this kind of fishing. His spider flies are simple, with a sparse but very soft hackle, whose fibres truly come alive in the current. They were the forerunners of the now well known "soft hackles", which can be said to represent the fish's food rather than actually imitating it.

The fish didn't have time to reject the fly. It was hooked with a lightning-quick strike and landed after a nerve-wracking fight.

Upstream fishing has several clear advantages, but also demands more of the fisherman. This is perceived as soon as you try it. For the current is a real problem here, as it brings the fly right back to you - and frustratingly fast, if you have not yet learned to control the loose line.

Nonetheless, you can then approach the fish from behind, where it is least attentive. And the fly is presented in the same way as the fish is accustomed to seeing food: drifting freely with the current. Even if upstream fishing is more demanding than downstream fishing, it is a far more effective method in trained hands.

The fly is laid with short casts upstream to the presumed holding places or observed fish. As the current brings it back again, you must take in the loose line and raise the rod tip, so that you always have full control over the fly and its journey through the water. With short casts, raising the rod tip while the fly drifts is sufficient - but with longer casts, loose line must be taken in as well. A long, soft rod of 9-10 ft (2.7-3.0 m) in class 5-6 is ideal for this exciting method, since you thus obtain the best possible line control.

The strike is made when you see the fish turn with the fly. Good eyesight is therefore essential. Here you do not have, as in downstream fishing, the chance to feel the fish strike - for the line is not taut. If you don't see the strike, the fish will almost always have time to spit out the fly. But if you are quick enough, the fish gets hooked even more solidly than in downstream fishing, where you cannot avoid occasionally pulling the fly out of the fish's mouth. So this is another advantage of the present method.

The method offishing a wet fly upstream is used mainly when thefish is very shy. It is also notably effective, since you are behind the fish and cannot frighten it as easily.

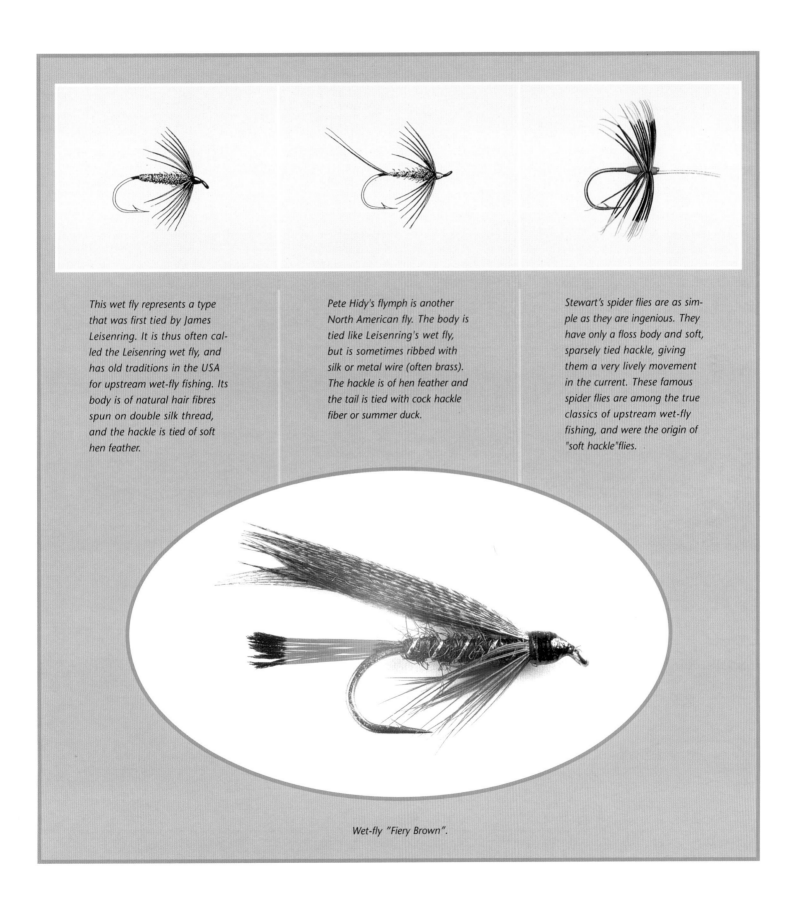

This wet fly represents a type that was first tied by James Leisenring. It is thus often called the Leisenring wet fly, and has old traditions in the USA for upstream wet-fly fishing. Its body is of natural hair fibres spun on double silk thread, and the hackle is tied of soft hen feather.

Pete Hidy's flymph is another North American fly. The body is tied like Leisenring's wet fly, but is sometimes ribbed with silk or metal wire (often brass). The hackle is of hen feather and the tail is tied with cock hackle fiber or summer duck.

Stewart's spider flies are as simple as they are ingenious. They have only a floss body and soft, sparsely tied hackle, giving them a very lively movement in the current. These famous spider flies are among the true classics of upstream wet-fly fishing, and were the origin of "soft hackle" flies.

Wet-fly "Fiery Brown".

Upstream dry-fly fishing

Although it was not Halford who "invented" the floating fly, this Englishman's name will forever be associated with the emergence of dry-fly fishing, which he systematized in order to make it an exact science. The purist members of his imitation school thought that dry-fly fishing with exact copies was the only proper form of the sport.

However, as we have already noted, this view soon developed into fanaticism. Imitations were tied of numerous insects - primarily mayflies - which occur on the southern English chalk streams, and these were imitations not only of the species, but also of both sexes and their stages of development in each species! The school went so far in many places as to ban all other kinds of fishing.

Dry-fly fishing is usually considered the most exciting form of flyfishing, since one can follow the whole course of events clearly. The advantage of upstream dry-flyfishing is that dragging flies can be avoided to some extent. The illustration shows this method with a curve cast.

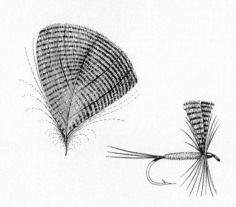

Dry flies of American type have soft wings from the flank feathers of ducks, mainly summer duck. Some well-known examples are the Cahill series, of which Light Cahill is perhaps the most renowned.

"Spent spinners" are mayflies that fall down dead on the water surface with outspread wings after laying eggs. The wings of their imitations can, of course, be tied with feather sections in the time-honoured way, but are increasingly being replaced by synthetic materials, and thus tend to be called "spent polywings". On spent spinners the tail and wing are separated into two equal parts with figure-of-eight tying.

A classic English dry fly. In this type of fly, the wings are made of quill sections. Some good instances are Black Gnat, Coachman, Greenwell's Glory and Blue Dun

Parachute-tied dry flies have the hackle tied in horizontally, wound around the wing root. Here, too, it has recently become ever more common to use synthetic materials in the wings, making "parachute-tied polywings". They can imitate a large number of species, and are thus quite handy and effective on many waters.

Some people regard dry-fly fishing as a simple, easy method. For the whole sequence of events is visible, in contrast to wet-fly fishing where, instead, you need a sort of "sixth sense" to tell you where and how to fish. Yet dry-fly fishing makes clear demands of good casting technique and line control. Whereas a few fish can often be caught by wet flies even with poor technique, dry-fly fishing is uncompromising in its own way. If you cannot present a dry fly lightly, elegantly, and at just the right spot - and if you cannot make sure that it floats freely over the fish without dragging, you won't get any fish. That's just how simple it is!

Dry-fly fishermen soon discovered the advantages of fishing upstream, and this method is still required on most of the classic English chalk streams. One locates a rising fish and sneaks up on it from behind, to within casting distance. The fly is placed far enough upstream so that the fish will have time to notice the fly and, hopefully, rise to it.

The main problem is "dragging" flies. These are dry flies that do not follow the current freely, but make furrows on the water surface. This is because the fly, leader and line do not drift with the same speed. When the fisherman stands on land or in the water, the current pressure on the line and leader will soon be transferred to the fly. It starts to drag immediately, no longer drifting freely like a natural insect, and is therefore usually rejected by the fish.

If you cast a dry fly straight upstream, this problem tends to be minimal. Then the current pressure is normally the same on the line, leader and fly, so they drift with the same speed as the loose line is taken in with your left hand.

Casting straight upstream to a fish that rises, however, will take the line and leader right over its head. This is bound to displease it and, in most cases, it will be frightened and stop rising. To avoid spoiling the opportunity, you should present the fly a little from one side. Lay it at an angle against the current, so that the line and leader do not hit the water over the fish.

As a result, though, the current will push differently on the line, leader and fly. If you leave it at that, the fly will very soon begin to drag, with greater pressure on the line than on the fly. But this can be prevented in various ways, with more or less advanced "trick" casts.

The simplest solution is to cast out a curved line instead of a straight, stretched one. Then the fly undergoes at least a short delay in floating freely downstream before the current

has stretched the line, and hopefully the delay will be long enough for the fish to take the fly. Casting a curved line is fairly easy. Most simply, the rod top is shaken from side to side when the line is stretched in the forward cast but is still in the air. This is commonly known as the serpentine cast.

It is much harder to produce so-called "curve casts". We speak of left-hand and right-hand curve casts, or positive and negative ones. The basic idea, of course, is to give the fly extra time to drift freely. Yet curve casts require such fantastic casting ability of the fisherman that most of us give up. They need training and a good understanding of the dynamics of the cast. Here we shall have to pass over these specialized techniques.

Grayling is a very popular quarry for flyfishermen in some parts of the world. In northern Scandinavia and the Alps, it can be tempted with a dry fly fished upstream.

Downstream dry-fly fishing

Fishing upstream with a dry fly can be justified on many good grounds, as we have seen - when the conditions are right for it. But by no means are they always so. Often a better method is to fish the same fly downstream, quite contrary to the classic and puritanical dry-fly school. Halford would turn in his grave if he could watch such a method being practised on his beloved chalk streams.

The English chalk streams, whose banks were the original cradle of dry-fly fishing, are relatively small and narrow waterways. They provide every reason to fish the fly upstream. Yet when fishing in larger and broader waterways, we frequently meet fish that simply cannot be reached by casting a dry fly upstream. It is then necessary to fish straight across the current, or even downstream, in order to get at the fish.

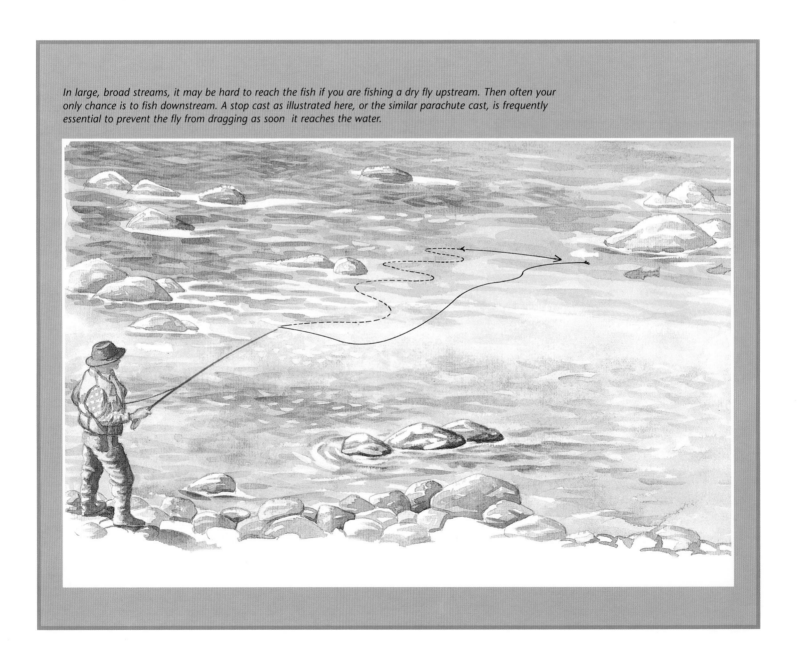

In large, broad streams, it may be hard to reach the fish if you are fishing a dry fly upstream. Then often your only chance is to fish downstream. A stop cast as illustrated here, or the similar parachute cast, is frequently essential to prevent the fly from dragging as soon it reaches the water.

Henry's Fork Hopper is a typical American grasshop-per imitation. Its body is tied with deer hair, and the wing with brown-speckled feather fibres. The deer hairs are folded backward at the head and clipped off on thefly's underside. These hollow air-fil-led hairs give thefly its excellent floating quality.

Here is another grasshopper imitation, loved by trout especially in the USA. This type of fly is cha-racterized by the Muddler head, tied with deer hair and trimmed to the right shape.

Bivisible is an example of a Palmer-hackled dryfly. The hackle is wound over the whole body, from tail to head. This fly can be tied in many colour vari-ants, but all have white hackle closest to the head.

Dry flies with bushy hackle are definitely good all-round imitations, and float very well even in fast currents. They are also easy to tie and to vary in colours. To be really effective, they are often tied with two hackles, wound in sequence.

Humpy is still another high-floatingfly for downstre-am dry-fly fishing It has a big bushy hackle of cock feather, as well as a tail and "body cover" of deer hair. This makes the fly float nicely even in strong current.

Goddard's Caddis was originally tied as an imitation of large caddis flies, but in the USA it is also used on waters where fish eat grasshoppers. It is tied mainly with airfilled deer hairs that make itfloat high, enabling it to rush across the water surface like a caddisfly or terrestrial insect in a hurry to reach land.

When fishing a dry fly across the stream, you may well have to mend the line upstream at intervals. Still better, though, is to learn the "reach" cast: after the cast has ended, but while the line is still in the air, you hold the rod upstream with an outstretched arm. Thus the dry fly receives a further delay before it begins to drag. Obviously the longer your rod and arms, the longer time the fly will spend drifting freely down towards the fish.

For fishing more directly downstream, the reach cast is not very helpful. Then you should use the parachute cast, whose name tells a lot about how it is done. Quite simply, the forward cast stops too soon, making the line stretch out while high up in the air. Holding the rod tip aloft, you let the fly line fall lightly and elegantly onto the water. The leader, which weighs almost nothing, follows passively along and comes down in a heap. This enables the fly to float freely a while longer, as you calmly lower the rod top and finish with your arms outstretched as usual.

The parachute cast is as indispensable for downstream fishing as the reach cast is for cross-current fishing. In both cases, you can lengthen the fly's free drift by releasing a few metres of loose line through the rod rings. For this to work, the line absolutely must be a weight-forward line, whose thin shooting line is easy to shake out.

As noted previously, fish take only the insects which are on the water surface within a rather narrow region overhead. If the cast is too long, downstream dry-fly fishing allows you to correct it by simply pulling the fly back into place! Once the desired path of drift is attained, you decrease the pressure and release some loose line. This must be done fast, since the line is now taut all the way to the fly.

The same technique can pay off when you need to skate a dry fly across to the fish. Until now, we have tried to make the fly drift as freely and peacefully as possible, and this is certainly the only good rule in most cases. But if, for example, there are big caddis flies, or insects that flutter about on the water surface, then a dragging dry fly is often the only thing that works.

Getting an upstream dry fly to drag realistically is out of the question. Natural insects invariably fight against the current not along with it. The current threatens to push them downstream, which they actively oppose. This behaviour is best imitated by fishing downstream with a dry fly that alternately drags and drifts freely.

The technique can be guided by raising the rod top with a taut line at intervals to release more loose line. But watch out - the strikes become violent when the fly is fished in this way. Here you need a controlled strike as well as a strong leader!

Strikes are relatively complicated, in either upstream or downstream fishing with a dry fly. Indeed they vary from fish to fish, and between different fishing waters. Thus, both fast and slow strikes can be useful in dry-fly fishing. Yet this can be quite frustrating to a beginner: the fly may be torn out of the fish's mouth, or will already have been rejected by it, if the strike is respectively too fast or slow. Luckily, there is a kind of system to follow. Calm fish should be hooked with a calm strike, and quick fish with a quick strike.

For instance, a trout that is holding in a quiet pocket on the edge of a strong current may be in a hurry to take insects on the surface. It shoots up, sucks in the prey and darts back to the depths. Naturally a dry fly will be taken in the same way, but since the fish is accustomed to a fast pace, it is quick to spit out the fly -so the strike must be made instantly.

The opposite is true of a fish that holds in calm water and sucks in spent spinners and other small insects. Knowing that it has plenty of time, it rises slowly to the surface and lingers confidently, sucking in the helpless insects. A dry fly is taken with equal laziness, and a fast strike would be sure to tear the fly out of the fish's mouth. Consequently, the fisherman must control himself – if possible – and delay the strike until the fish is on the way down with the fly. This can be as difficult as it is exciting!

These two general situations are easy to deal with in practice, as we can decide in advance which type of strike should be used. However, one is often forced to make the choice during the strike itself, and that may be even harder.

In calm waters, the fish sometimes makes a side-detour. to take a good morsel which it has seen from a distance. It has to hurry, and its strike is more violent than usual. The same happens if the fish rises at the last moment for a poorly placed dry fly which drifts far to the side. We may have decided in advance that this particular fish requires a calm strike, but now we must make a new decision in a fraction of a second! Similarly, if the fish takes hatching insects that can lift from the water at any time, it may act speedily and require a quick strike.

In general, small fish are fast and big ones are slow. So the rule of thumb is that big fish should be given more time to

In downstream dry-fly fishing, you can easily imitate the insects that fight against the current, by raising and lowering the rod tip. This allows the fly to drag against the current at the surface, or to drift freely a bit downstream. The fish may then take violently when they no longer can stand the temptation.

take the fly and descend with it. This can be difficult to follow in practice - especially if you have been fishing all day for small trout and grayling, which call for quick strikes and may make you unable to change your style. If you then happen to confront the biggest fish of the day, or even of the year, it is worth taking a pause. But once the situation is clear to you, there should be less trouble in adjusting. You can always close your eyes and count to three as the fish takes the dry fly!

Finally keep in mind that, if the fish takes the fly on a long cast, the strike must be made faster than usual. The longer your line is, the longer time it needs to transfer the strike to the fish. Conversely, with a short line you can hook the fish at a more relaxed pace.

Nymph fishing

While puristic dry-fly fanaticism was at its height along the southern English chalk streams, a prominent lawyer strolled by those waters, deep in fresh thought. Professionally he was accustomed to reasons and logical proofs - an ability which he extended to his observations on the fishing waters.

G. E. M. Skues became the next pioneer of flyfishing. He realized that the trout in his chalk streams did not by any means always take the winged insects on the surface even if Halford wished that they did! Quite often, the fish instead took nymphs just under the surface.

These facts led Skues to tie the first true nymph flies. They not only sank like wet flies, but were also imitations as exact as the dry flies of that time. With them, he fished precisely as though they were dry flies; the only difference was that they were presented freely drifting under, or in, the water surface. Such "wet-fly fishing" did not appeal to Halford and his disciples. As a result, Skues had to struggle for years before his method was accepted as a worthy alternative to dry-fly fishing. As luck had it, he succeeded.

The next step towards modern flyfishing was made by Frank Sawyer, a riverkeeper on the River Avon. His job

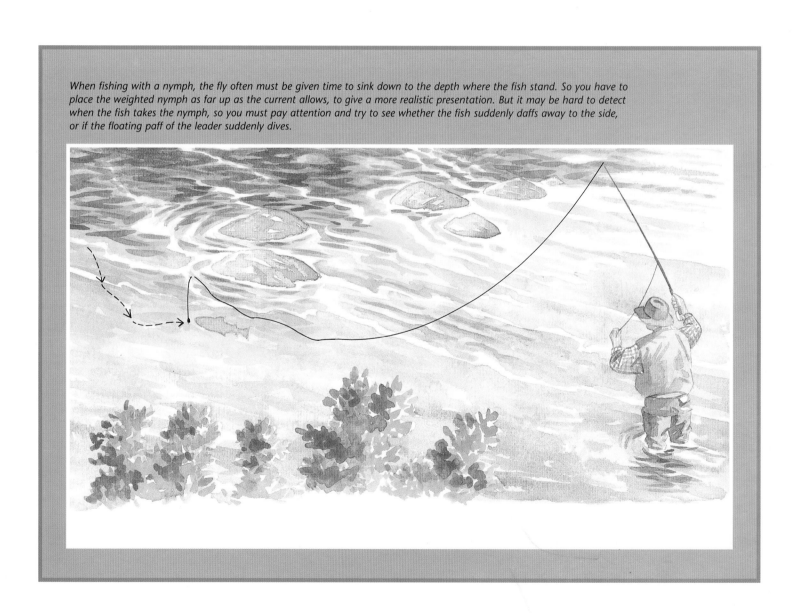

When fishing with a nymph, the fly often must be given time to sink down to the depth where the fish stand. So you have to place the weighted nymph as far up as the current allows, to give a more realistic presentation. But it may be hard to detect when the fish takes the nymph, so you must pay attention and try to see whether the fish suddenly daffs away to the side, or if the floating paff of the leader suddenly dives.

afforded much time to study fish in their natural element Thus he discovered that the trout were often active along the bottom, when no activity was occurring at the surface. Obviously the fish consumed food, so they ought to be catchable.

Just as Skues tied his nymphs as imitations of fully developed mayfly nymphs, Sawyer created the astonishingly simple Pheasant Tail Nymphs, representing smaller nymphs that were not yet fully developed like adults. He had noticed that these always held their legs to the body when swimming. For

the same reason, in contrast to Skues, he omitted the hackle from his flies. Instead, he weighted them so that they would sink quickly to the bottom and, therefore, to the fish. Sawyer fished his nymphs upstream towards observed fish, without making any extra movements.

Oliver Kite, also a denizen of the Avon, developed this technique further with his "induced take". If the fish will not take a freely drifting nymph, the cast is repeated and the fly is lifted up in front of the fish's nose - like an escaping insect. And not many fish can resist that!

This is a type of nymph which imitates stonefly nymphs. It comes from the northwestern USA, where it is very popular in fishing for cutthroat trout, rainbow trout and brown trout. The body is often a combination of dubbed material and plastic strips in different colours. The wing cases are of either plastic or tied-down feather sections, the tail and antennae of stiff fibres. Usually it is weighted or tied on a heavy hook.

This Skues nymph is tied with a sneck-bend hook and shows how Skues himself tied it. The nymph has a small dubbed rear body with a conspicuous dubbed breast section, but also soft antennae and a soft hackle. It must not be weighted, as it is usually fished in the upper water or in shallow currents.

Frank Sawyer's classic Pheasant Tail is a very simple but effective fly. It imitates small, not yet developed, nymphs. The fly is weighted with copper wire to sink fast to the bottom, and is thus well suited to upstream nymph fishing, since it must be fished without any extra movements.

Here are two types of caddis-fly with dubbed bodies. These bind microscopic air bubbles to themselves, giving them a silvery appearance like the hatching insect. The imitations can also be provided with "lively" wing cases or hackle, and the body can be ribbed with wire. Such flies may be fished at all levels in the current, depending on how much they are weighted.

In almost every way, nymph fishing is a cross between dry-fly and wet-fly fishing. You can fish upstream or downstream, with a floating or a sinking line. The flies vary from the biggest to the smallest, and are fished underwater like wet flies, but are tied as pure imitations like dry flies. Such a range of variations is enough to confuse even the most zealous beginner at flyfishing.

There is, however, a certain system in the methods and their use. Pure upstream fishing can be done only when the current is not too strong. Under calm conditions, you can fish with a floating line, long leaders and weighted flies. You cast to observed fish or presumed holding places. At all events, the aim is to place the nymph so far upstream of the fish, or holding place, that the fly has time to sink to the right depth.

Once the nymph is at the fish's level, the problem is to detect a strike. This is easy enough if you can see the fish and fly clearly. If only the fish is visible, you must watch for it to make a quick turn aside, when the fly is presumed to be nearby. The white gape of the fish's mouth is a sure sign that it has taken the fly or a natural insect. Whatever happens, you must tighten the line instantly, so that the fish will not have time to spit out the fly. It may hold a very small nymph in its mouth for a long while, and then it is usually hooked well - all the way down in its throat.

If you see neither fish nor fly, you can only rely on the visible signs at the water surface. The line tip or the leader's floating - possibly greased - section may suddenly be drawn under the water. Life is definitely made easier by using a "strike indicator", consisting of a little cork ball, a piece of foam rubber, or a stub of poly yarn. This works like a float and reacts immediately if the fly is taken. Its location along the leader depends on the fishing depth.

Upstream nymph fishing with a floating line and a long leader can be done with any size of nymph. If you choose to fish downstream, you must remember that only relatively large, powerful insects are able to fight against the current. Small mayfly nymphs have no chance, so it is understandable why the flyfishermen on the classic chalk streams always fish their small nymphs of size 14-16 upstream. Anything else would involve an unrealistic presentation of the fly.

Notably active and strong swimmers are the big caddis fly pupae, which like to oppose the current. Therefore, imitations of them can be fished downstream to advantage, meaning nymphs of size 8-12. According to the current, they are fished

When a large trout takes drifting midge pupae in the surface layer, often only its back fin and paff of the back appear above the surface.

with a floating, sinking, or sink-tip line. Here a sink-tip is preferable to a fully sinking line, since like a floating line - it allows regular mending of the line, which in turn enables the fly to fish correctly. Just as in ordinary downstream wet-fly fishing, the fly should not normally drag.

In really strong currents, nymphs must be fished upstream, using strong equipments, a fast-sinking line, a short leader and large weighted flies. The flies are usually imitation stoneflies of size 2-8. As such fishing is a little violent, its practitioners are not very numerous. The fly is transported upstream with short casts, enabling it to sink before it passes right in front of the fisherman. While the line is sinking, the curent pulls it away, so the point is to hold as much as possible of the line out of the water as the fly sinks. This is best done by holding the rod top high with outstretched arms.

If everything else has been done right, the big nymph will have reached the correct fishing depth when it is just in front of you. Only then does it begin to fish. You must therefore let the nymph drift freely over the bottom as far as possible, by

lowering the rod top at the pace of the fly's drift. Most fish take when your line and arms are stretched downstream, since the fly then starts to climb and swing out of the stream. The strike feels violent in the hard current, but the fish is often poorly hooked. Thus a certain percentage of fish is always lost by this method, but it is still the only one that works well in strong currents.

Finally, a word about the rather unusual form of nymph fishing which occurs each summer in Alaskan rivers. It uses so-called "roe flies" that imitate, in colour and form, individual fish eggs. During the summer, thousands of Pacific salmon migrate up these rivers to spawn and die. On the journey upstream, they are accompanied by grayling, Arctic char, and rainbow trout - which intend to eat the roe left by the spawning salmon. This annual drama is a fascinating sight. Like small grey-black shadows, the roe-eaters flit. among the large salmon at the spawning grounds. When the female salmon releases some roe, they dash forward and partake of it, before the male salmon chases them away.

As the salmon are so plentiful, the roe is a very important supplement to the diets of other fish in the rivers. For the same reason, roe flies are extremely valuable to the flyfishermen who swing their rods in Alaska during these periods. The round, fluorescent flies should not be missing in any fly box!

Roe flies are fished exactly like the nymph fisherman's other imitations, by "dead drift" right over the bottom. Normally you can get by with a floating line and long leader, but in some reaches of water it can be necessary to fish with a sink-tip line. As a rule, the current is strong just over the spawning bottoms.

These flies can be weighted so that they sink quickly to the fish, but then they do not sway freely with the current. So it is better to weight the leader - by fastening lead shot to one of the blood knot's loose ends, or winding lead wire round the leader just above the lowest knot. The fly will thus come down to the bottom and, at the same time, drift freely with the current. This approach can also be used to advantage with any other nymphs.

Streamer fishing

Fishing with streamers and bucktails is both the easiest way of flyfishing, and the method that yields the biggest fish! This may sound paradoxical, but it isn't. There are two reasons: you can do nothing wrong with a big streamer or bucktail, and the fact is that big fish prefer big flies.

Streamers and bucktails represent various small fish, and are tied on long-shanked hooks. In addition, they may be pure fantasy creations. A streamer is tied with soft feather-wings, of saddle hackle or marabou, and it is intended for fishing in relatively small and calm waters. By contrast, bucktails are provided with hairwing - originally hair from a deer's tail, hence the name - and they are consequently suitable for fishing in broad, fast waters. Historically, streamers belong to the American east coast, while bucktails come from the west coast. But apart from that, they are fished in the same way.

The nice thing about small fish compared with tiny insects and crustaceans is that, to a great extent, they can oppose the current. Being strong swimmers, they commonly dare to enter more open and rapid water. As a result, the flyfisherman can fish his flies almost anywhere he likes: up or down or across the stream, either fast or slow. The fly will be equally attractive in all cases, and you need not worry about whether the fly will drag. At the same time, with big flies, we address the largest fish in the water, which of course are notorious fish-eaters. Really large fish have long ago given up eating small insects in favour of more substantial young fish. Otherwise they would never have reached the size that makes them so desirable to us!

Trout are the commonest guests of our fly rods when we fish with streamers and bucktails. Grayling prefer insects and other small creatures, although this does not prevent large grayling from occasionally taking a small streamer. When it comes to trout, one can get the feeling that not even the largest streamer is large enough.

The great majority of small fish in flowing waters are definite bottom-dwellers. This applies not least to the minnows - already mentioned - and the sculpins, which exist in many fast rivers around the world. They not only live on the bottom, but actually spend most of their time resting on it.

All this means that the flyfisherman's long-shanked flies should be fished as deep as possible, with a sink-tip or fully sinking line. Only in the smallest, shallowest waters can you get by with a floating line. On the other hand, you can fish rather daringly with these big flies: fast or slow, upstream or downstream. There are unimagined possibilities of variation, in contrast to the usual fishing with wet flies or nymphs.

It is more than a matter of using your imagination. If the fish does not take a freely drifting streamer, try instead taking home the line very quickly. Now and then you can even "awaken" a lazy trout by letting the fly splash down right on top of its head. One must admit that this is not an elegant manner of flyfishing, but it can be extraordinarily productive.

Normally we fish streamers and bucktails as imitations of the small fish that exist in the given waterway. They are tied, and fished, with maximum realism. However, the usefulness of these long-shafted flies hardly stops there. They are also effective in provoking the waterway's spawning fish to strike.

As noted in Chapter 2, trout are aggressive fish that defend individual territories in the stream. They are aggressive all year round, but this behaviour becomes ever more manifest as the spawning time approaches and they defend their territory with fury against any intruder. The flyfisherman can take advantage of this situation when the fishing season is coming to an end and the trout's spawning time arrives. Then the fish may be hard to attract with ordinary imitation flies since, having feasted all summer, they are fastidious and well-nourished. Besides, they are ever less interested in food and increasingly concerned with spawning.

It is then time to serve a big, colourful streamer or bucktail - a fly whose size and hue can, by themselves, give the fish an impression that some possible rival is encroaching on its territory.

This method of fishing can be pretty exciting. It is important to have a good knowledge of the locality, so that you know exactly where the fish are holding. You have to seek them out with streamers and bucktails of large size, and present the fly right in front of them repeatedly until they react. Often nothing happens on the first cast, so you must continue stubbornly. For the more glimpses the fish gets of the fly, the more irritated it becomes. Finally it cannot endure the temptation and tries to chase away the fly.

Right: Big fish gladly take big flies. Towards the end of the season, when trout are no longer so interested in small insect imitations and try to defend their territory more actively, a streamer or bucktail can be quite effective.

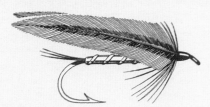

In recent years the word "streamer" has wrongly come to mean all flies tied on long-shanked hooks with long featherwings or hairwings. A traditional streamer, however, has only wings made of long hackle feathers, tied in at the head. The body is often of floss or flat tinsel, ribbed with oval tinsel.

Bucktails, as the name implies, were originally tied with deer-tail hair. But today they are tied with various types of hair, for example from calf tail, squirrel tail, polar bear or goat. The body is tied, just as in a streamer, off loss and/or tinsel - the wing and hackle being tied in at the head. One may also tie in a tail of coloured or plain feather fibres.

Thunder Creek is an American type of fly meant to imitate small fish fry. Since the food of fish can vary around the world, this fly should be tied in the colours that best resemble small fish in your own water. The wings are tied in three steps: a thin bucktail wing on the hook shank, bent backward; then a dark bunch on the upper side and a light bunch on the underside, both pointing forward; finally the bunches are bent backward and fastened with tying thread.

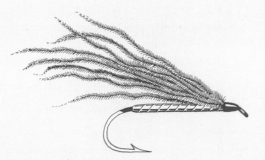

Long-shanked hooks of streamer type, with maraboufeather wings, have become ever more popular. The advantage of this amazingly soft wing material is that it gives a lifelike impression in the water, often attracting fish to take. Such wings create little air resistance, so you can swing out rather large flies even with a relatively light-actioned rod.

It is typical of Matuka streamers that the wing feathers are wound along the whole body. The fibres on the undersides of two hackle feathers are removed, and the wing is placed on top of the hook shaft and fastened at the head. Then the ribbing is wound carefully forward through the wing and is attached at the head. Finally a false hackle is tied in.

The rainbow trout - whose seagoing variant is the steelhead - belongs to those species that gladly take a well-served streamer or bucktail.

At first you frequently feel only a strong blow against the fly, without hooking the fish. The fly has thus only been hit, not taken in the fish's mouth. Yet there is a good chance that one of the following casts will result in a solid strike by what may be the season's largest trout. In any case, such fishing is fascinating once the quarry has been aroused.

In Alaska and British Columbia, every year sees a rather special kind of streamer fishing for large rainbow trout and Arctic char. It takes place when extensive schools of salmon smolt begin their migration downstream toward the Pacific Ocean. They are often smolt from sockeye salmon, which emerge from lakes in the water system - of which the predatory fish are well aware. So the latter gather at the outlets of lakes to feast on the young salmon. If you stumble upon such a smolt migration, you are sure to have exceptional fishing experiences for quite a while. Sparsely dressed streamers and bucktails are the only thing worth putting on your leader.

In several places farther north, trout are regularly caught with mice or lemmings in their stomachs. These small rodents provide the fish with huge chunks of concentrated protein, yielding a colossal spurt in growth. Thus, during good years for mice and lemmings, they are the sole diet of many large trout, and you need to "match the hatch" by serving a delicious deer-hair mouse that floats on the water surface. This mouse is fished dragging, and the fish takes it with a savage strike.

An important point is to fish near the banks, where the fish are accustomed to seeing mice or lemmings tumble in. Big flies are required, so you have to give the fish plenty of time to take the fly before tightening up on the line. Otherwise you will only tear the mouse out of its mouth. Whoever has tried this fishing once is sold on it for a lifetime!

If you fish a deer-hair mouse in quiet parts of a stream, it is often attacked by pike, which offer an entertaining sort of fishing. Pike are not distinctive stream fish, and avoid the fast sections of a waterway, but they can be abundant in sections with deep calm water. Here you may also find small schools of perch that gladly take a little silvery streamer.

Catch and Release

Whatever the method of fishing, stocks of fish in streams are fairly vulnerable. The quantities of food, and therefore also of fish, are strictly limited. In addition, every waterway has only enough holding places for a certain number of fish, especially when they are trout. As a result, we obviously cannot catch more than a small number of fish in small streams, and then only if the streams are in their natural condition.

Today, most waterways are far from being in as good condition as they should be. Damming, regulation and pollution have gone mad among them. In many places, this has meant that no natural reproduction exists any longer. A lot of waters contain only stocked fish. Thus a natural waterway with natural fish stocks is an extremely valuable resource that should be treated with great care.

Rational fish management, in the latter case, is not conducted by harvesting any surplus, but by protecting the fish that are there already. The best approach, of course, is to leave the fish in peace - with no sportfishing. But the next best, and most realistic, is to put back the fish that are caught. This policy is what Americans call "Catch and Release", or "No Kill".

"Catch and Release" is undoubtedly the future basis of fishing management. With a steadily rising pressure on our fishing waters, there is no alternative, unless we degenerate to plain "put and take". Sportfishermen simply cannot afford to continue harvesting the last stocks of wild fish.

"No Kill" is not a form of snobbery, as many Europeans unhappily believe. It is a rational form of fishing management that has been used professionally in the United States for the past 10-15 years, and with good results. There, most fishing is open to whoever has obtained a fishing licence in the given state. Only in a few places is fishing subject to private ownership as in Europe.

This status has made possible a coordinated, more effective fishing management in large water systems, as well as a test of "No Kill" and its effects on a suitably large scale. The American fishing authorities can, whenever they think necessary, impose new and stricter regulations for a particular fishing area. They can immediately raise the minimum size, decrease the allowed number of fish caught, put a waterway under protection - or introduce "No Kill".

The whole process has been gone through in the United States. It began with virgin waters that offered fabulous fish-

ing to the relatively few sportsmen of those times. There were plenty of fish, and big ones. Yet after World War II, the fishing pressure really began to grow, and many such waters were fished out. The authorities set out quantities of new fish, and once again there was a quarry to catch. This was straightforward "put and take" fishing. Next, however, critical voices

These stretches soon became popular, since big fish were still to be found there, offering a real challenge to the more demanding sportfishermen. At the same time, many scientific studies showed that the natural fish stocks were growing healthily under this radical form of fishing management. "No Kill" spread subsequently to numerous other waters.

There is no point in introducing "Catch and Release" if flyfishermen do not know how to handle the fish that are caught. All too many will die after being released. But if the fish are handled properly, they will quickly regain strength - and be able to give some other fisherman a lively experience later on. As Lee Wulff once expressed it: "A trout is too valuable to be caught only once!"

The following rules should therefore be followed when releasing fish:

– Use barbless hooks, which make the releasing much easier. They hook the fish better than ordinary hooks do, and are still a lot easier to remove. Press down the barb, file it off, or use true barbless hooks. If a barbed hook sits deep, clip off the leader near the hook and leave it there; the fish will then get rid of it.

– Fight the fish as quickly as possible. This prevents the formation of too much lactic acid in the fish. Never use a leader which is thinner than necessary for this. Super-thin leaders are not "sporting": rather the opposite.

– Let the fish stay in the water as long as possible when the hook is to be removed. Never touch the fish with dry hands, which can injure its protective layer of mucus. Use a landing net of knotless cotton, which is most gentle for the fish. If the fish is to be photographed, hold it with one hand by the tail and the other hand under its front body. Be careful not to squeeze the fish, and never touch its gills!

– Revive the fish before releasing it. Hold its head upstream in flowing water, or move it back and forth in still water, so that fresh water passes over its gills. Not until the gills pump regularly again, and the fish can keep its own balance, is it ready for releasing. The fish should be able to swim out of your hands by itself.

spoke up. People did not want to have fish regardless of the price. They wanted quality fish - born in the wild and raised in natural waters, not in fish farms. It took a long time before the authorities reacted, initially with stronger restrictions on fishing, and later by introducing the first clear "No Kill" stretches on special waterways.

Fishing for salmon and sea trout

I would compare salmon and sea trout to a half-sleeping cat which lies down in the sunshine and pays little attention to its surroundings. Of course, unlike the salmon, a cat will feed when it is hungry, but at times it is provoked to attach something that it has no intention of eating- such as a leaf blowing in the wind. Some reflex action is triggered by the sight of a moving object and induces the cat to chase it. This may have less to do with the object's colour than with its movement, and possibly its resemblance to a small prey.

However, many wild cats survive by being able to run fast, and must be continually on the alert - even practising when they are not feeding. Fish, particularly salmonoids, rely on their speed of interception to get a meal. Possibly on occasions they take a fly when their reflexes have been triggered to attack something that they neither want nor need as food.

Thus, before fishing for salmonoids, it may be very important to learn not only how to cast well, but also how to think and act like a hunter, and to study animals in order to acquire a sense of their behavioural rhythms. One can even make notes of the feeding times of birds, fish and animals such as cattle and sheep. With trout and other fish which feed in fresh water, it is worth observing their feeding times and diet. We cannot directly do so with salmon and sea trout, but we must be aware of the rhythms of wildlife - as well as getting to know the water that we are fishing in.

The future of salmonoid fishing

Another general point to remember is that the future of the wild Atlantic salmon species is severely threatened today. Our fishing should therefore be conducted responsibly, which may mean a limit on catches and the methods of catching. The late British king George V summed it all up by saying: "The wildlife of today is not ours to dispose of as we please. We have it in trust and must account for it to those who come after us."

There is still a great magic in seeking salmon with a fly, and the thrill of the take never pales. Yet unless conservation measures are applied, we may have already lived through the golden years of salmon fishing. Surely mankind will not be so foolish as to let this sport slide into obscurity through wanton neglect!

Throughout most of Europe, the two main species of anadromous fish, Salmo salar and Salmo trutta, are better known

by their common names: salmon and sea trout. But the prefix "Atlantic" must be added for salmon, while the European sea trout is perhaps better identified as a sea-run brown trout. This enables us to distinguish them from the five species of Pacific salmon, belonging to the genus Oncorhynchus, and from the sea-run rainbow trout known as the steelhead.

The majority of flyfishermen consider the Atlantic salmon to be the leading sportfish. With experience of many species of salmon and sea trout, however, I am not sure that this accolade is well-deserved. The fresh-run sockeye and coho salmon in Pacific rivers are hard fighters, as is the steelhead. And where else in the world would you find salmon that grow to the size of the chinook or king salmon, nearly 100 pounds (45 kg)?

The techniques of angling for salmon originated largely in Europe. Much of the folklore that has grown up around salmon was created by the British. Not only were they in the vanguard as sportfishermen for salmon, but their influence and expertise contributed a great deal to developing the Scandinavian resources.

Above: *Good casting technique, and long experience on the same river under varying conditions, are typical attributes of a successful salmon fisherman.*

Left: *Atlantic salmon – the ultimate challenge for many flyfishermen.*

Equipment

There are still numerous countries in which many forms of angling are permitted. Nonetheless, many of us feel that fly-fishing not only offers a greater challenge, but also represents a better sporting method of catching these lovely fish. It is now several years, for instance, since I have fished for salmon with any other lure than a fly. On many rivers the methods of flyfishing can be very effective, although on a few rivers they are less productive than certain forms of bait-fishing.

It is, then, angling with a fly that will occupy us here. This is a superb way of enjoying sport with worthy fish and once you have mastered some of the basic techniques, it is much easier than might be supposed by beginners.

Much of the tackle used in flyfishing for salmon and sea trout was invented in England. About 150 years ago, backbreaking rods of up to 20 ft (6 m) were fashionable. Leaders were of plaited horsehair and twisted silkworm gut. The most dramatic changes in tackle have taken place since World War II. Today carbon-fibre (graphite) has ousted glass, split cane, greenheart and hickory as rod-building material, while reels have become far lighter and more effective.

Silk lines and twisted flax are virtually things of the past. Modern synthetics give us every required combination in floating and sinking lines. The Association of Fishing Tackle Manufacturers (AFTM) has standardized much of this tackle, so that specific line sizes and weights can be made compatible with rods. Perhaps the greatest benefit that synthetic fibres have brought is in the field of transparent monofilament. Based on nylon, it has eliminated the need for gut or horsehair casts, and some remarkably high breaking strains are produced with minimal diametres.

Traditionally the fly rod was, and still is, double-handed. It may be anything from 12 ft (3.7 m) for fishing a river of modest size, to 17 ft (5.2 m) for a broad river. Much of the flyfishing in Britain and Scandinavia is done with double-handed rods. But North American anglers, who often fish from canoes, have shown a marked preference for the single-handed rod. At least one noted American angler, Lee Wulff, takes great delight in extracting massive salmon on a toothpick-like fly rod of only 6 ft (1.8 m) weighing less than 3 oz (85 g).

Patience, watchfulness and powers of concentration - these are qualities a salmon fisherman needs.

The choice of tackle

In making your initial choice of tackle, however, it is important to decide where you will do most of your fishing, and at what time of year. A lot depends on your location and the size of the river. A Norwegian river in June, for instance, may be nearly at flood level from melting snow - whereas a river of similar size in Scotland or England may already be thinning down to summer level, long after the main snows have melted.

The best choice for spring fishing on Scotland's famous river Spey, and in large Norwegian rivers during summer, is a 15-ft (4.6-m) double-handed carbon-fibre rod. With this I would carry at least two reels: one with a slow-sinking shooting-head line of size 11, and the other with doubletaper fully floating line of similar size. The DT line is almost essential in order to do a proper Spey cast, while the sinking shooting-head line may be cast overhead for long distances. I would also carry a range of flies varying from 2.5-in (63 mm) tubes to size 6 or 8 doubles or trebles, without much concern for pattern.

One can also bring a net, gaff or other implement to extract fish from the river. Many prefer to wade the river with as little encumbrance as possible. For early spring or late autumn in Scotland, and during the summer in Scandinavian rivers, good tackle includes the following items:

- A stout pair of felt-soled breast waders, preferably in neoprene.
- The 15 ft (4.6 m) double-handed fly rod.
- Drum fly reels of 3.75 x 4 in (95 x 102 mm) with adjustable drag.
- A 30 ft (9.1 m) shooting-taper slow-sinking line of size 11, and another of fast-sinking type, attached to oval monofil backing.
- A 30 yd (27 m) double-taper floating line of size 11, spliced to at least 150 yds (137 m) of 25 lb test backing.
- A big box of flies, as outlined here.
- Spools of nylon monofil, between 10 lb and 25 lb test.
- A pair of scissors.

Additional accessories could be a wading stick, net gaff, and so forth. Indeed, if you do not know your river intimarely, it makes good sense to have a wading stick. This should have a weighted bottom, so that it is always at hand and does not float on the surface. If floating, it can make trouble and foul up some of the line which you intend to shoot.

As an alternative and back-up outfit, for such fishing in early spring or autumn, I recommend a single-handed rod of about 10 ft (3 m) with a smaller fly reel, and a forward-taper line of size 7 with an 8 lb test leader. This is a much-loved outfit for late spring and summer fishing on the small or shrunken streams of Britain. Moreover, it is fantastic fun to play a salmon on a light, single-handed rod. And there can be little doubt of the tactical value of such an outfit when the rivers have shrunk to their bare bones, with fish that are shy of all but the most slender leader.

An important aspect of tackle selection and use is your mastery of the best knotting techniques. All knots cause a loss of strength in your leader, and bad knots can be so inefficient that they may reduce the strength by more than half. It is a good idea to learn knots so thoroughly that you can almost tie them blindfolded.

One of the worst knots that may accidentally be induced into your leader is politely known as a "wind knot". Sometimes it may occur in very windy conditions, when the leader gets tan-

When fishing in deep and rapid waters, you should use a short leader, since the pressure of the current lifts up the leader and fly to the surface.

gled and a single overhand knot is produced. This makes the leader extremely fragile to sudden loads, and might well break it when a fish is being played. Such knots can be termed "bad casting knots", since they can usually be avoided. All you need to do is open up the loop of the line a little, and lower the rod tip immediately after the power stroke in the forward cast.

Selecting flies

Most discussion of the effectiveness of salmon and sea trout flies is speculative. Since the fish do not feed after returning to fresh water, they may have no interest in whatever we offer them, and no strict logic will tell us what size or pattern of fly will be the best in any given circumstances.

However, salmon can indeed occasionally be caught on a wide variety of fly patterns. Ancient lore suggests that we use big flies in extensive, deep and cold waters - and small flies in limited, shrunken rivers when the water is warmer and the fish are confined to shallower areas. In practice, there is a whole range of techniques which defy the basic rules, although we should never be dogmatic about them.

It is wise to arm yourself with a wide variety of fly patterns, in varying weights and lengths. Sometimes the weight of the fly is more important than its overall size. At other times you may want as small a fly as you can find Generally, there is a lot to gain by having as large a selection as can be carried comfortably.

For fishing in early spring on many of Britain's classic rivers, I use a heavy sinking line and a tube fly, mounted on brass tubing to enable it to sink well down in the water. If the river is full with melting snow or recent rain, it may contain some suspended matter and thus lack the crystal clear quality of a river at normal height. In addition, the water temperature may be a little above freezing, and this could be an occasion for the large fly if fished as slowly and deeply as possible.

Alternatively, the same river in late May or June might need little more than a light floating line, and a singlehooked fly of size 10 or 12 which is lightly dressed and has little weight or drag effect. Still, there are no fixed rules, and I have frequently seen a complete reversal of tactics bring about an unexpected success.

In making your choice of fly pattern and size, it pays off to keep in mind the laws of nature. Nothing in the wild which is preyed upon by other species has a garish appearance. The prey usually has some form of natural camouflage and does not look out of place in its environment. This fact should dictate the choice of fly in very clear water. Do not select a fly which is conspicuous, and it is a good idea to make your flies ever more subdued in colour as they get smaller. In high turbid water, however, you may well need to confront the fish with a more garish lure - and perhaps even intimidate the fish, presenting the lure where it will threaten the fish on an eye-to-eye collision course.

THUNDER & LIGHTNING

Tag: oval gold tinsel
Tip: yellow floss
Tail: golden pheasant crest feather
    and Indian Crow
Butt: black ostrich herl
Body: black floss
Ribbing: oval gold tinsel
Body hackle: orange cock hackle
Front hackle: blue guinea hen or blue jay
Wing: brown feather sections from
    brown mallard
Topping: golden pheasant crest feather
Sides: jungle cock
Head: black

This is how a classic salmon fly is tied Thunder & Lightning is a good example of dark flies, which work best by evening and night or in bad weather (hence the name?) and when the water is murky.

At right is shown a Silver Doctor. This lightfly is most suitable in fine weather and when the river water is clean and clear. It belongs to the Doctor series and is also a good instance of a Mixed Wings fly.

The colour of flies

On the above basis, I find it helpful to use a colour of fly which matches the overall colour of the riverbed. Some rivers are generally brown, like weak coffee without milk, and these call for a dark-brown or black fly. The Spey responds well to this type, and patterns such as the Monro Killer, Thunder & Lightning, and Stoat's Tail are all effective. Other rivers, for example those flowing off bare rock or limestone, are often crystal-clear at times of normal flow, absorbing much ultraviolet light. They may have a blue or green tinge, making flies of the same hue more suitable.

During early spring and late autumn, though, your river will probably be higher than normal, and unusually turbid due to rainwater. I would then recommend slightly brighter or garish flies in yellow or orange for very cold days, and less conspicuous flies for warmer days. Good examples of flies for high, cold water are Yellow Dog, Tadpole, Willie Gunn and Collie Dog.

Nonetheless, the final act of deluding a fish into taking your lure is often unrelated to your choice of fly pattern. It may have something to do with the size of the fly, but usually the decisive factor is how you present the fly. Unfortunately, a fisherman who accepts the advice that he is fishing with the wrong fly might become furious at the suggestion that his casting and presentation are poor. In spite of that, the tactical and technical requirements are most likely to cause failure. And if there is a prerequisite in salmon and sea trout fishing, it is knowledge of the best techniques needed for any given situation.

When choosing a fly, you should naturally take into account its size, colour and dressing, but the presentation is often what determines whether the salmon will take.

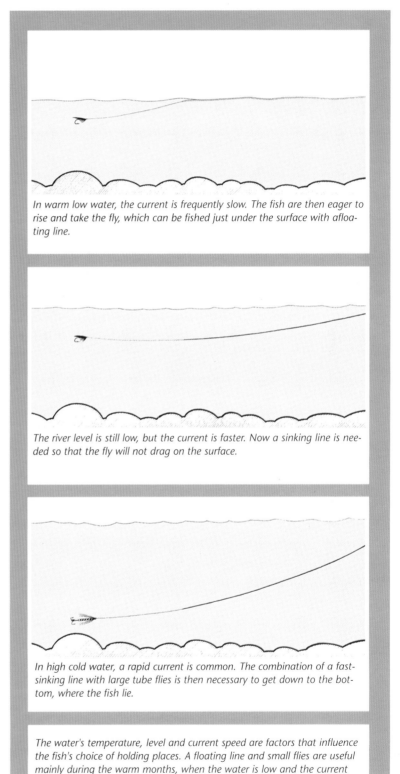

In warm low water, the current is frequently slow. The fish are then eager to rise and take the fly, which can be fished just under the surface with a floating line.

The river level is still low, but the current is faster. Now a sinking line is needed so that the fly will not drag on the surface.

In high cold water, a rapid current is common. The combination of a fast-sinking line with large tube flies is then necessary to get down to the bottom, where the fish lie.

The water's temperature, level and current speed are factors that influence the fish's choice of holding places. A floating line and small flies are useful mainly during the warm months, when the water is low and the current therefore slow. But in the early season, with high and cold water, the current is strong and the fish take the fly at a greater depth. You must then often fish with a fast-sinking line and large flies.

Casting and presentation

Experience shows that this kind of fishing depends mainly on the ability to cast a long line and on intimate acquaintance with the water being fished. The one-week-per-year salmon angler is severely restricted, and his difficulty is compounded if - like so many of us - he likes to try a different river each year. At no time will he ever fish a single stretch of water and get to know it under all its conditions. Yet he will never be able to fish it to full potential until he has tried for several years on the same stretch.

It is not intended here to teach the complexities of casting. A videotape may be more helpful than a book, but the best way to learn is from a professional instructor - not an enthusiastic amateur, however talented - and to spend as long as is needed to master the techniques under his supervision. Anglers often spend surprising sums of money in fishing rents, travel costs and hotel bills, only to prove themselves incompetent at casting when they arrive at the water.

For double-handed fishing, you must be able to cast at least 25-30 metres (80-100 ft). Such distances may not be achieved immediately, but it should not take long to accomplish them comfortably in the overhead mode. It is then very important to master both the single and double Spey casts. These will enable you to fish areas of water that are obstructed by overhanging trees or high banks, and where the overhead cast is impossible.

Letting the rod work

The novice should learn that it is the rod which must do the work - and that style, not brute strength, will make the cast look good and be effective. Ladies and small men often seem to be better stylists, while large and powerful men apparently work hard but do not achieve the right distance or style. But if you have both style and strength, you may well be on the way to becoming an exceptional salmon fisherman!

If you have no experience at all, it will pay to begin with a double-handed rod and a floating line. This gear is more quickly mastered than the single-handed rod or a sinking line, although the techniques are basically the same. The rod must act as a spring when casting, and as a lever when playing the fish. Thus, to get the best from your rod, you must use its springiness - and this is where many problems occur.

Some fishermen simply wave the rod about, using more

Above & opposite: *An experienced salmon fisherman knows that he must let the rod do the work, if he is to fish for a whole day with a long double-handed rod. Every cast has to be as energy-saving as possible.*

muscle than they need. It is the flex of the rod that propels the fly line. No matter how much energy you expend, if you merely wave the rod and do not load it as a spring, you cannot cast far or with great style. Good casting is not an art, but a craft that any able-bodied person can soon learn.

The next difficulty, getting access to good water, has already been mentioned. Direct access to the best waters is not easy, even if you can afford the rent. But it is wise to get the best you can, and to remain a regular tenant over the years until you know the best times of year and the best places for fishing. Such knowledge is not easily won, either - and that is why many of the classic salmon waters have gillies, or guides, to assist the visitor and ensure that he fishes only the most productive areas.

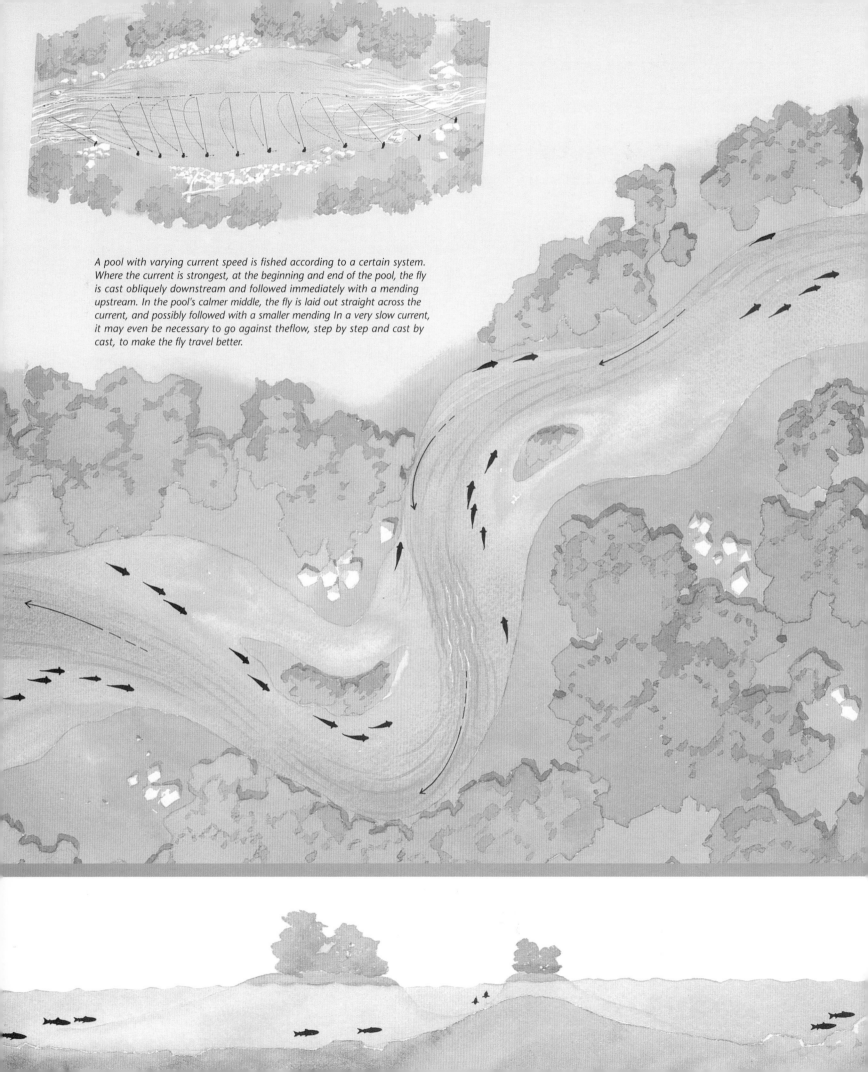

A pool with varying current speed is fished according to a certain system. Where the current is strongest, at the beginning and end of the pool, the fly is cast obliquely downstream and followed immediately with a mending upstream. In the pool's calmer middle, the fly is laid out straight across the current, and possibly followed with a smaller mending In a very slow current, it may even be necessary to go against theflow, step by step and cast by cast, to make the fly travel better.

In shallow flowing parts of a river, fish often lie before or beside large stones or cliffs, where they can find lee from the current.

A stretch of river is illustrated here in top view and cross-section. As can be seen, the fish prefer to lie at the inlets of pools - gathering their strength for the next stage of migration - and to rest at the outlets after having overcome previous obstacles. In long wide pools, though, the fish try to lie in the outer edges of the current.

The taking times

At least one British salmon writer has observed that it is impossible to overfish a salmon river. What he meant was that it is not easy to put fish permanently into a non-taking mood, and that they may always - at some time of their own choosing, for some unknown reason - suddenly "come on the take" and grab the first lure they see. In any case, we must evaluate the condition of the fish. A fresh fish entering a new lie for the first time, and taking a brief rest, may be quite likely to snatch at the first thing to antagonize it. Until we know why salmon take our flies, we are naturally only speculating - but experience shows that fresh-run salmon are very vulnerable in this respect, and that many are caught when running without staying long in a lie. Here I feel that it is almost impossible to overfish the lie or the river. But where the fish have run into holding pools and stayed for some time in a lowering water, it does seem possible to over-intimidate them into a non-taking mood.

There are undoubtedly many instances, in salmon and sea trout fishing, where "familiarity can breed contempt". Moreover, what can we gain by continually flogging a stretch of water when there is a total lack of response? It may make better sense to rest, as well as giving the fish some respite.

The idea of resting a stretch of water, of course, poses hard questions. On many rivers, it is impossible to tell exactly what is happening under the surface. Only by having a fish-counting device at the inlet and outlet of every pool could we determine just what stock it contains from one minute to the next. But since the stock is often a matter of pure speculation, it may be that resting a pool will reduce the chance of familiarity breeding contempt. Indeed, the next time your fly is shown to the fish, some new stock may have moved in, or one of the old residents may have changed its mood.

It is not strictly true that one can never predict the taking times of the fish. Those that settle into lies for several weeks are known to be residents. You may even recognize some of them by the positions in which they show, by their leaping style, and by their size or colouring. However, it is important not to overfish for them - and to fish at times when "all of nature is in tune", as suggested by a knowledge of the behaviour and feeding times of other animals.

Although salmon and sea trout are known to be nonfeeders in fresh water, some memory of their heavy marine feeding may trigger a reflex and make them respond at some times of the day better than at others. One of the most predictable

taking times, throughout the season and in any kind of weather, is the last hour of daylight.

The weather in Scotland may vary greatly during April and May. One day might have air and water temperatures around 5-8° C (41-46° F), while another may have the air at 15° C (59° F) and the water at a magical 10° C (50° F). In any event, when fishing with a fully floating line, it is very important that the air be warmer than the water. Choose a day when the opposite is true, and you may well draw a blank.

As emphasized above, the angler who does best with salmon and sea trout is usually one who lives on, or near, the river he is to fish. He gets to know all its moods and whims, ignoring the temptation to try a new river every year. For this reason, I am now reluctant to try new waters. Age does not leave me enough time to learn them as intimately as I know, for instance, the Castle Grant beat of the Spey, or the Upper Floors beat of the Tweed.

Left: The salmon has taken the fly, yet many long and dramatic minutes remain before it can be landed.

Below: A salmon often rises calmly and slowly towards a fly in the sub-surface. If it decides to take, which is far from certain, it usually does so heavily and decisively rather than violently.

How to tie a tube fly is shown here. The example is Garry, an all-round pattern that has proved to catch salmon throughout the year, but is perhaps most effective in the early season when the river water is at a high level and low temperature.

GARRY SPECIAL

Tag: oval and silver tinsel
Butt: black ostrich herl
Tail: golden pheasant crest feather
Body: black floss
Ribbing: oval silver tinsel
Body hackle: sparsely tied black cock hackle
Front hackle: blue guinea hen
Wing: red and yellow bucktail
Head: black

Practical flyfishing

Suppose that you are fishing early in the season, and the river is at nearly perfect height, with a water temperature of around 4° C (39° F) or perhaps a bit warmer as in Scandinavia. You are using a 15 ft (4.6 m) rod, a sinking line, and a garishly coloured 2.5 in (6.3 cm) tube fly. Taking up a position that enables you to cover the lies, you make your first cast.

Initially a few short casts should be made toward the opposite bank, pulling a yard or two of line from the reel at each cast, until you have enough line out. But it should be remembered that a longer cast will allow the fly to get farther down in the water- and that by holding up the rod tip, immediately after the cast, you will keep more line off the water as the fly begins to swing, so that it will sink farther.

Do not be in too much of a hurry to strip back line for the next cast. Let the fly dangle for a few seconds, then casually pull in the first two or three loops of backing. Sometimes during the cold weather of the early or late season, fish will slowly follow the fly and take it only as it is being withdrawn upstream. On occasion, especially in the autumn, my fly has been snatched while hand-lining back at full speed.

These slow tactics offer the best chances in cold weather, but it may be useful to speed them up a little as the water warms. However, salmon - notably the Atlantic salmon react much less quickly than sea trout, which can grab a fly and take you down to the backing in a single rapid movement. Besides, Atlantic salmon differ in behaviour from the same species in North America, which often display real pyrotechnics. All Pacific salmonoids, particularly when fresh-run, are fairly savage on the take, whereas the more ponderous Atlantic salmon of the early spring are rarely willing to snatch and flee like summer sea trout.

In sink-line fishing, you should always try to hold the rod high. As seen in the upper illustration, the fly then has a chance to sink properly toward the bottom. If the rod is held too low, as in the picture below, too much of the line will float on the surface due to friction, keeping the fly "hanging" a little under the surface.

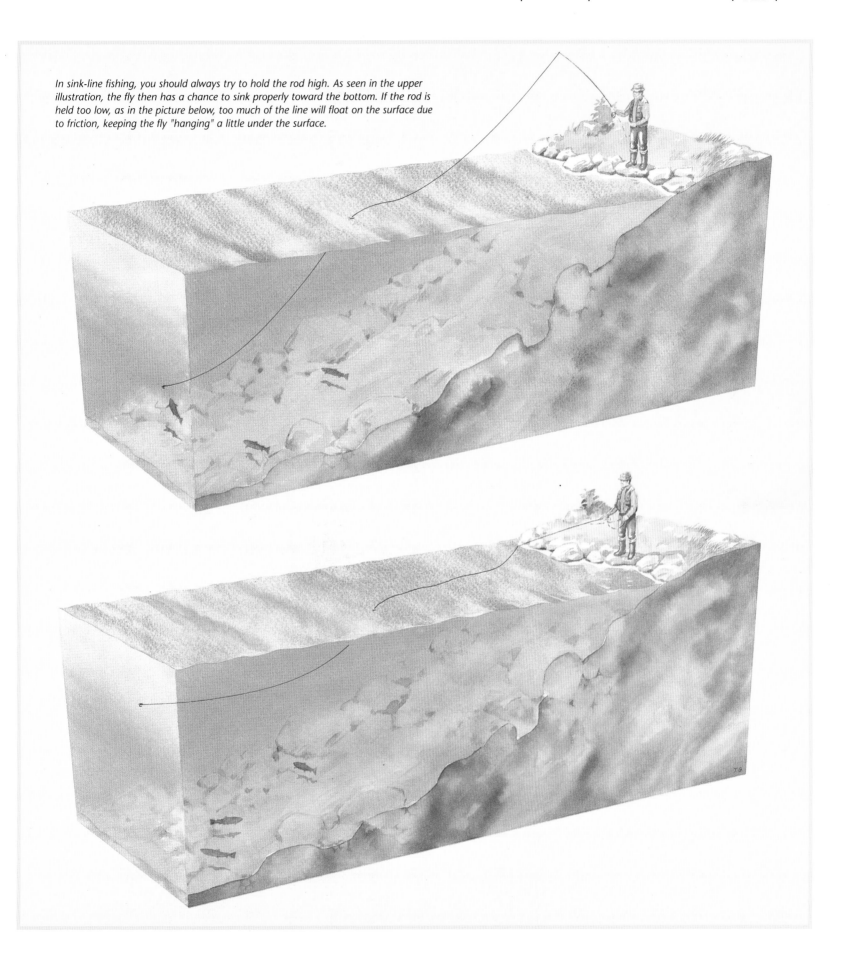

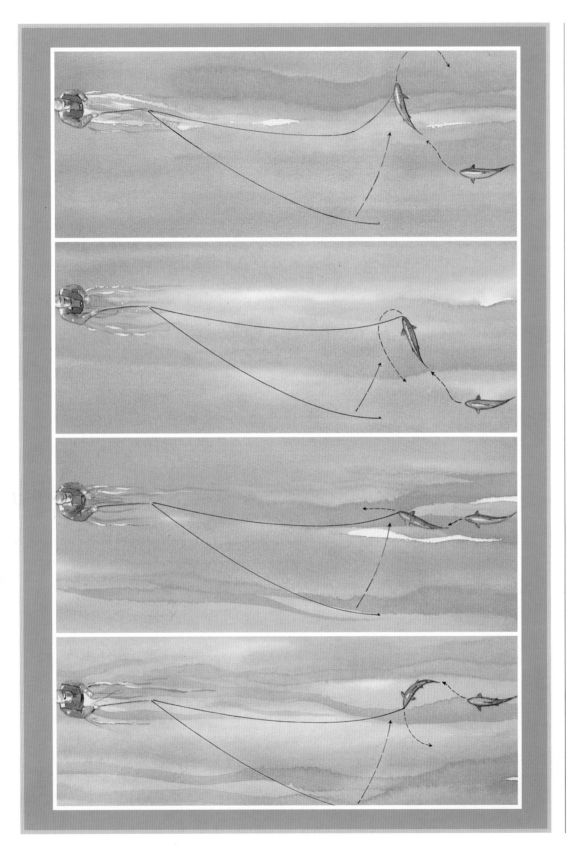

Salmon can take a fly in various ways, and opinions on what to do after the take are almost as numerous as salmon fishermen. Shown here are four common ways for salmon to take. The fish nearly always rises upstream to inspect the fly and possibly take it. Then the fish usually falls back with the current in some direction. Only in the third example does the fish continue upstream after taking the fly.

Though the fish often hooks itself you should always make a clear strike as soon as you feel it on the rod. No matter how it takes the fly and how you hook it, you should let it work against the rod during the whole fight. Give it as little chance as possible to rest, ideally by playing it in the faster part of the current.

Opposite: Will the salmon take the fly - and if so, how?

Hooking and landing

There are several opinions about what to do when a salmon takes the fly. Some anglers, especially those who have read a great deal on the subject, seem to be obsessed with feeding line to the fish at the moment of the take. Others, who may have caught a lot of fish, apparently believe that you should hold hard when you feel the fish and let it hook itself. The present writer prefers the latter view. Possibly a fish in very cold water will get hooked on any slack line fed to it, but I see no reason to do this at any other time. I agree with the idea of holding hard, or even striking, at the instant when the fish is felt pulling on the rod tip.

Exactly what you do after hooking the fish depends to some extent on its mood. It may soon take the initiative and do unexpected things, such as rushing away downstream and threatening to break the line. But usually it stays in the pool where it was hooked, so you need only give line when it pulls strongly, and win back some line when you feel it trying to rest. The fish should be kept active, and preferably in the fas-

ter current. Do not let it get so far downstream that it can lean on your tackle to resist the current.

But neither should you stay opposite the fish simply in order to keep a side-strain on it. This might lead you far downstream from your starting point. Normally I like to play and land a fish from the place where I was standing when I hooked it. Naturally there are times when you have to move, but a good rule is to stand fast.

Before long, in fishing for salmon or sea trout, you will realize that certain conditions must be met if you are to catch fish by design rather than by accident. The angler who has got to know the water in all its moods - and who has learned to cast far - will, in the long run, score heavily over the inexperienced novice. Yet perhaps the main requirement is a "command" of the water. What counts is not merely casting out to the fish, but being able to make your fly move over the fish in such a way that it is more likely to be taken than refused. Achieving effective water command is possible only with expert advice from your gillie, guide or boatsman, unless you have long personal experience of the water you are fishing.

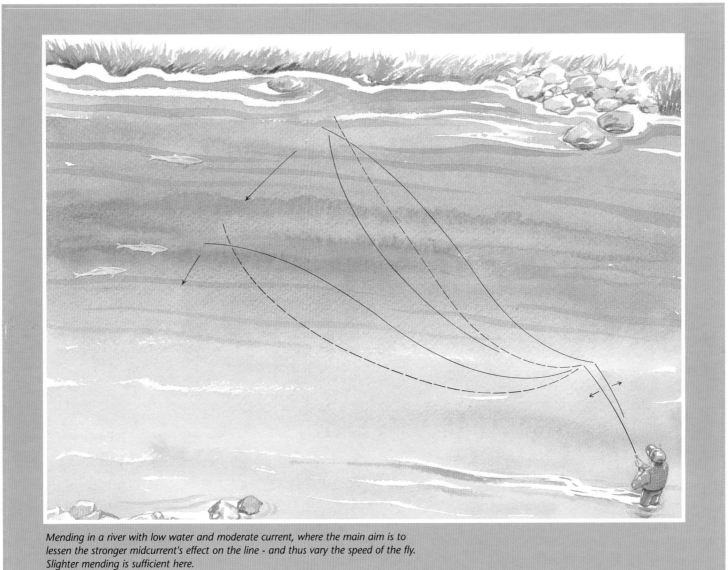

Mending in a river with low water and moderate current, where the main aim is to lessen the stronger midcurrent's effect on the line - and thus vary the speed of the fly. Slighter mending is sufficient here.

Mending the line

One of the first lessons a salmon flyfisherman should learn, particularly if he is to fish mainly with a floating line, is the technique of mending the line. This refers to the movement which you give the line after it is cast and has fallen on the water. Normally a sinking line cannot be mended significantly, so it is important to make a good straight cast that will minimize the central current's influence on the line.

Of course, when fishing a river with a floating line, you are always casting across flowing water where the current's strength varies from one side to the other. Often the central current forms a "belly" in the line, and - as shown by the illu-

strations - this gives the fly an unnatural movement. A very strong central current may cause so much belly that the fly is whipped round in a fast-moving arc, which is frequently quite unattractive to the fish.

But by switching the line upstream, mending its belly formation shortly after it has fallen on the water, you can slow down the fly and enable it to swing round more gradually. Sometimes the current speed varies widely – and the angler who can continually read the situation, mending or modifying the curves in his line, will have greater success than one who merely casts the fly across the flow and leaves it to fend for itself!

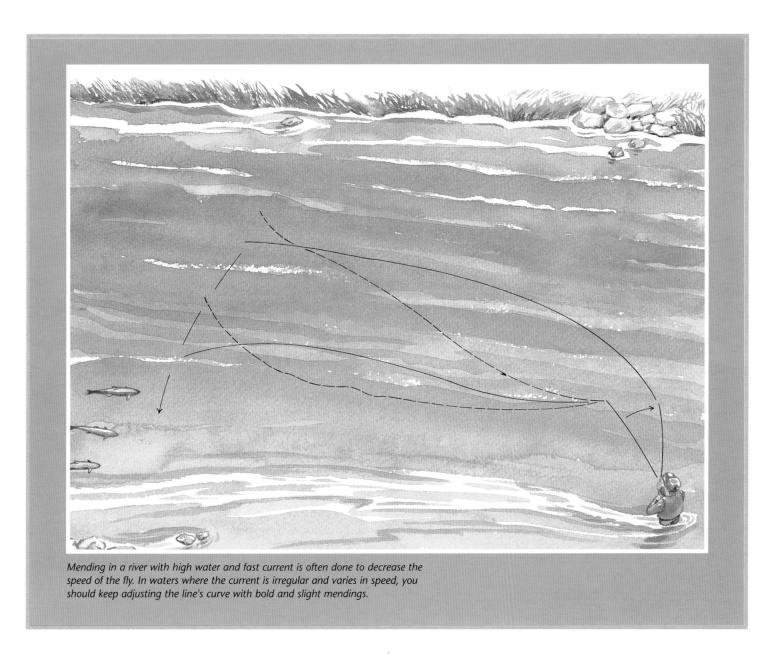

Mending in a river with high water and fast current is often done to decrease the speed of the fly. In waters where the current is irregular and varies in speed, you should keep adjusting the line's curve with bold and slight mendings.

In general, a longer rod improves your chances of creating effective mends. Especially on fast water, an upstream mend is often needed to slow down the fly. But sometimes, in very sluggish water, a downstream mend may be best. This increases the belly in the line, giving the fly more movement and speed to make it attractive.

When fishing with a sinking line, however, there is very little time in which to mend the line. If a sinking line is to be mended at all, this should be done just after the cast, before the fly and line can sink down in the water.

An understanding of the degree of movement which your fly must have in relation to the current, and thus the speed and angle at which it should be fished, will come only with experience. As already noted, a fly that passes too quickly over a lie may not incite the fish to take, while a fly that passes too slowly may be recognized as a trick or may fail to trigger the fish's attack mechanism.

Besides, what triggers a suitable response at one time may not do so at another. There are also variables of air and water temperature and clarity, climate, barometric pressure, oxygen content, and the general mood of the fish at a specific time of day or night. All of these add to the possibilities, and it is still true that no perfect formula can ensure the downfall of fish.

Methods

There are various distinctions between methods of salmonoid fishing. The most common methods on the British, Scandinavian and North American rivers are fishing with a sink-line and with a floating line. The former is most effective when the river is high and cold, whereas the latter is best for a low warm river.

In addition, numerous other approaches are used according to the conditions at hand. For example, on North American rivers it is normal to fish for salmon with a dry fly and a technique called "riffling hitch". In parts of the Scottish highlands, local methods such as "dibbling" are very popular. Large rivers like the Tweed in Scotland, and the Alta in Norway, tend to be fished best from a boat, as when harling.

Fresh-run fish

During the early season, the prime time for salmon fishermen, you can expect to catch some of the freshest fish of the entire season. Some of these may be bearing sea lice the hallmark of fresh-run fish. It is assumed that sea lice can survive in fresh water for only 48 hours, but they have been known to do so for up to seven days under laboratory conditions. Even then, a fish with sea lice must be regarded as excellent, both for sport and on the table. However, you may get a poor fight from a fresh-run fish, especially when the water has warmed a little and when the fish may have run a long way in a short time. Such fish might be already partially exhausted from their swim, needing several days to get back into prize-fighting trim.

Another fish that may be encountered during the early months is called a kelt. This is an Atlantic salmon which entered the river during the previous year and spawned already during that autumn. Not all such fish return quickly to the sea. Many die, as do all the Pacific salmon species and other kelts linger in fresh water, not returning to the estuary until March or April, particularly after a hard winter. Kelts are recognizable by their lean and lanky appearance, ragged fins, and distended vent. One should also look for maggots in gills, and not be fooled by an overall silver appearance - somewhat like that of fresh fish. Such kelts are merely in the process of donning their seagoing coat.

When hooked, a kelt does not normally fight as hard as a fresh salmon. But well-rested kelts may prove to be more

stubborn fighters than is generally appreciated. The law in several countries is that all kelts must be returned to the water, although there are instances in North America where it is permitted to keep them. In any event, they are fairly useless as food.

Late spring salmon

Some Scottish rivers are famous for their early runs of salmon in January, February and March - a period often curiously called "spring" by anglers. Others become better for the sporting angler when spring turns into summer, from April to June. This is the heyday of the flyfisherman who enjoys fishing with a floating line, and when wading is more comfortable, with a general sense of spring in the air. There may still be lots of snow on the mountains, and a strong flow of water in the rivers - but for many of us, this is the peak of the season.

During the past few years, I have almost given up the early season so that I can concentrate on the latter period of better weather. This is a wonderful time to be alive on many of Scotland's classic rivers. Although the spring run on several of them is no longer as prolific as it was thirty years ago, the stocks build up gradually as summer arrives, and the big migrations of fish often do not come until late summer or early autumn.

However, in many other countries with stocks of Atlantic salmon, the season tends to be much shorter. In Norway it is confined to June, July and August, while in Iceland and North America it is more or less the same.

The salmon could not resist the fly, fished with a single-handed rod and a floating line.

Salmon can be caught at any time from early spring to late autumn, but nothing beats an early summer salmon in May.

Summer fishing

One basic difference between Scotland and Scandinavia, as regards fishing, is the size of fly to be used. In Scotland during June, most of the snow has already melted and the rivers are fining down to summer level. A similar river in Norway or Iceland, however, still has a large run-off of meltwater; although the sun is high and air temperatures may be above 20° C (68° F), the water may be little more than 5-8° C (41-46° F). Often, therefore, the Scottish angler who is fishing water around 15° C (59° F) uses flies of smaller sizes (8-12) while the Scandinavian fisherman is still using big tubes and trebles up to 3 in (7.5 cm) long - the type used in Scotland during February and March.

Tactics in Scotland at this time may involve fishing mainly in the early morning and late evening. Certainly little can be achieved by fishing over low water on a hot sunny day when the air temperature soars over 20° C (68° F). Even in Norway, where the fresh fish are then entering the rivers, it might pay to delay your main effort until the sun has sunk behind the lofty mountains - or even, in the region which enjoys the midnight sun, to defer all fishing until evening and continue through the night. Some of the northernmost rivers, such as the famous Alta, are fished only between 6 PM and 6 AM.

Fishing for sea trout

Although salmon and sea trout have been treated above as similar species, they differ subtly in behaviour, and sometimes so much that entirely different tactics are needed when fishing for a specific species. Certain writers even suggest that the two types of fish cannot be related when discussing tactics. However, in reality you will often catch sea trout when fishing for salmon, and vice versa.

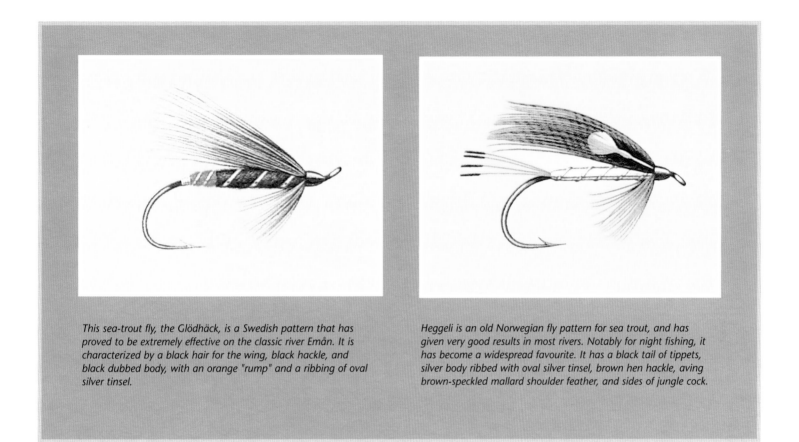

This sea-trout fly, the Glödhäck, is a Swedish pattern that has proved to be extremely effective on the classic river Emån. It is characterized by a black hair for the wing, black hackle, and black dubbed body, with an orange "rump" and a ribbing of oval silver tinsel.

Heggeli is an old Norwegian fly pattern for sea trout, and has given very good results in most rivers. Notably for night fishing, it has become a widespread favourite. It has a black tail of tippets, silver body ribbed with oval silver tinsel, brown hen hackle, aving brown-speckled mallard shoulder feather, and sides of jungle cock.

Below: A sea trout usually takes the fly near or in the surface. The fly should be fairly small, size 6-10. Unlike salmon, sea trout actually feed also after starting their spawning migration, so they tend to take decisively and can seem quick, even violent.

A single-handed rod is the commonest choice for sea-trout fishing, just as for salmon fishing in North America.

Sea trout, particularly those that have been in a river for some time, are very shy. On their first run into fresh water, they may be quite easy to catch - but after only a short interval, it may turn out that they can only be caught at night. In midsummer, on the rivers of northern Europe, this may mean starting as late as 10 PM or so.

On normal waters, you should usually begin with a single-handed rod and a floating line, using flies of sizes 6-10, and fishing in the traditional style - casting across the current and letting the fly swing round. The water's sporting potential will tend to be indicated by the amount of surface activity among the sea trout. Takes are often savage, and the fish present some huge thrills as they charge about, trying to throw your hook. Such sport may last until midnight and complete darkness. But sometimes a dead silence falls, leading you to conclude that the fish have gone down and ended the game for the

night. However, this may be only a "half-time" pause by the fish, so that you can take a brief rest and resume fishing - with a sinking line and a big lure as long as 3 in (7.5 cm). This "second half" may be just the time to catch the larger sea trout, and you may be able to continue fishing until dawn.

Nights with a cold wind, or air colder than the water, should be avoided. Moonlight is not advantageous. The best nights are those with balmy breezes from the south-west, a little moisture in the air, and a myriad of insects dancing in the shadows of late evening. Sometimes, later in the season, the darkest nights offer the best sport of all.

Yet at other times, it is frequently possible to catch sea trout along with salmon. Despite notable differences in tactics, sea trout may respond in much the same manner as do salmon. Indeed, although salmon rarely take after dark, it happens on rivers like the Spey that a fish is caught in late evening and you

Pacific salmon

Of the five principal species of Pacific salmon known in western North America, the most important for sportsmen are the chinook, or king salmon (also called the tyee in parts of Canada), the coho or silver salmon, and the sockeye or red salmon. The others, the pink and the chum salmon, are plentiful but not very interesting for sport, and make only low-grade canned salmon.

My experience of fishing for these species has been confined to Alaska. There I have found that the coho, sockeye, and chinook can provide exceptional flyfishing when they are fresh-run. It is rare to see anyone using a double-handed rod, and only occasionally might one be needed. A light single-handed rod of 9-10 ft (2.7-3.0 m) is usually sufficient. Balance this with a floating line of size 7, sometimes with a sink-tip, and a test leader of 8-10 lbs. Then you can have some super sport, particularly with the coho and sockeye. The chinook does not respond very well to small flies, so it is advisable to use a sinking line and large lures, on extra strong leaders of 20-25 lbs, in case you tangle with a monster weighing over 50 lbs (23 kg).

Much the same techniques as with Atlantic salmon are used for fishing with a floating line. But it pays to go very deep for the chinook, and to fish as slowly as possible. The fight from a chinook is about the same as from big Norwegian salmon, although it lacks the same lustre and cannot be compared on the table. Perhaps the highest gourmet marks are earned by the fresh-run sockeye. Indeed it is this species, when caught at sea, which goes into expensive cans of "prime red salmon". None of the other Pacific species get beyond the "pink salmon" label.

The most popular sea trout on the west coast of the United States is the sea-run rainbow trout called the steelhead. Among the most highly favoured by American flyfishermen, it is reckoned to be the "fightingest" fish on that continent. Many of the biggest specimens are taken with bait-fishing techniques, but a flyfisherman can get good results with large flies on sinking lines.

Dry flies are often used for salmon fishing in North America, and when fishing for sea trout in a few Norwegian rivers. Among the best known dry flies is the Wulff series, created by Lee Wulff. Here we see Grey Wulff, which floats very well due to its tail and wings of hair, and to its bushy hackle of cock feathers.

GREY WULFF

Tying thread: *black*
Tail: *bucktail*
Body: *dubbed grey wool*
Wings: *bucktail*
Hackle: *grey cock hackle*

do not know what it is until you have netted it. Usually I do not care whether it is a salmon or a sea trout, for both are equally welcome on the table!

Salmon are commonly caught with dry flies in North America, but rarely in Europe. At times a dry fly is very effective for Scandinavian sea trout, even in the middle of the day - yet salmon can seldom be induced to succumb. Only a few times have I caught salmon on a dry fly which was intended for trout, and there have been a few more occasions when I caught sea trout.

Saltwater flyfishing

Tackle has improved dramatically. Rods for graphite are available that are light enough even for women to easily cast, making it comfortable to fish with larger and stronger tackle, which is often needed to subdue these powerful fish. Reels developed just for salt water are now so over-designed that they will handle far more than will ever be demanded of them. Fly lines have improved, with special ones developed just for saltwater use. In the world of fly patterns there are now several hundred, where a few years ago anglers only used several dozen basic flies. Even the materials that today's saltwater patterns are made from have changed. Vast improvements have occurred.

For many Europeans shut off from fishing private waters in their countries, and for other fishermen around the world who see their fresh waters deteriorating or disappearing, flyfishermen are looking to other areas where they can enjoy their sport. Salt water offers unlimited opportunities for this. Flyfishermen can effectively catch fish in waters to about 60 ft (20 m) deep with new tackle and flies. In waters less than 10 ft (3 m) deep, fly tackle is often more effective than other types of artificial lures. In very shallow waters (2 feet or less) realistic flies can be presented so quietly that often the flyfisherman can catch fish better than someone using any other tackle, or even bait! This is especially true with wary species such as bonefish which, when feeding, will frequent waters so shallow that their dorsal fins often protrude above the surface. Under these conditions many fish are extremely wary and will flee at the slightest splash of a lure or bait. The silent entry of a fly is often the best way to present to such fish.

Great fighters

Salt water also offers other bonuses. Most fish sought by fly rodders in fresh water do not have many predators. The fish they seek are at the top of the food chain and it is they who are doing the chasing. But in the sea, nearly every fish is being eaten by another that is larger and more fierce. While some bottom-living species, when attacked, can retreat into a cave or under a rock, most saltwater species can only escape by going away. And they must swim faster and farther than the predator or they will be eaten. Such an environment produces fish that are much superior to freshwater fish, as far as speed and endurance are concerned.

All of this is a plus to the flyfisherman. When the hook is set in most saltwater species (other than some bottom-living types), the fish give a far better fight and run off more line than almost any freshwater species. The first time an angler hooks a 5 lb (2.3 kg) bonefish and watches the line melt from his reel as this relatively tiny fish pulls off more 100 yards (91 m) of backing in that first burst of speed, he cannot believe that it is the same fish that took his fly. To battle a tuna, trevally, large mackerel, or any swift open-sea fish is a delight and surprise to the angler who first hooks one of these speedsters. And because of their strength and speed, special tackle is often required to subdue these fish.

There are two basic kinds of flyfishing in the sea: inshore and offshore. Inshore waters are those within about a half mile (1 km) or so of the coast, and usually not more than 12,5 ft (4-5 m) deep. Waters deeper than that are generally regarded as offshore, and usually require different tackle and different fishing techniques.

In colder seas, such as off the coasts of Europe and the northeastern and northwestern United States, flyfishing is not productive for much of the year. Even when it is, generally the numbers of species and times that you can catch them on flies are limited. There are some bottom species in all of these estuaries that will take a fly; mackerel, bluefish and some other species may appear during warmer months. But the most exciting world of saltwater flyfishing is confined to waters where temperatures in the sea rarely drop below 60 degrees and often are 80 degrees or warmer. The closer one gets to the equator, the more opportunities exist for year-round flyfishing. In these warmer seas, food is abundant all through the year and there are many predators that take flies. Many of the species that inhabit these warmer oceans in cold weather will migrate briefly north and then return as the water temperatures drop.

Opposite: Sharks belong to the true big game of the seas, and can be caught with flies in many parts of the world. Offering a long hard battle, they are superb to play on a fly rod.

Flyfishing inshore

When fishing the shallows, two basic approaches are taken. In very shallow, clear waters, such as the flats along the coasts of Africa, Florida, the Bahamas, Yucatan and islands in the south Pacific, many species of fish live in slightly deeper waters, but move into the shallows to feed. Such species include the famous bonefish, permit, tarpon, snook, trevally, threadfin salmon, barramundi, snappers, groupers and channel bass. Much of this is sight fishing, among the most interesting of all kinds of fishing. The angler either wades or else is propelled in a boat (usually with someone poling it) across the flats (shallow saltwater areas are often called flats); it is a combination of hunting and fishing. Both the angler in the bow of the boat, armed with a fly rod, and the person poling the boat are looking for fish. Once the fish is seen, the poler attempts to position the boat so that the angler can make a productive cast. This hunting/fishing offers great appeal to many fishermen, and is a major reason why tarpon, bonefish and permit are among the most publicized and popular of all species sought with a fly rod in salt water.

Noticing the fish

Sight fishing, and knowing how to look for and see fish in the shallows, require some skills. Fortunately, most of them are easy to master. First, the angler needs the proper equipment, so that he can see. A hat is essential, preferably one with a dark under-brim. This cuts down glare reflected from the water and allows the angler to see much better; hats with bright under-brims reflect the glare from the water into the eyes. The other piece of equipment that helps the angler's vision penetrate the surface is a good pair of polarizing glasses. These help to remove most of the glare from the surface. While it is a personal choice, most experienced "flats fishermen" prefer brown or amber-tinted glasses, rather than gray or green-tinted ones. The brown or amber builds contrast and makes it easier to see these fish. It should be remembered that tarpon, bonefish, permit and many other species have silvery sides, which act much like a mirror. When a tarpon, whose back is dark green, swims over light sand it is very easy to see: the back stands out against the light sand. But when the same fish cruises over dark-green turtle grass, it becomes very difficult to see. This is true of all flats fish that are silvery in colour.

Fortunately, there are some skills you can learn that help you to see fish with mirror-like sides. You look for any fish swimming in very shallow water differently than when they are moving in deeper water. A fish swimming in water less than 1 ft (30 cm) deep will create wakes, ripples and small swirls on the surface. Indeed, some fish stand on their heads to root out a bit of food. This means the tail may protrude above the surface, so the angler should look intently at the surface. Anything that moves will instantly be noticeable.

When the fish are in water deeper than that, the angler should look at the bottom. If you look at the surface, you will

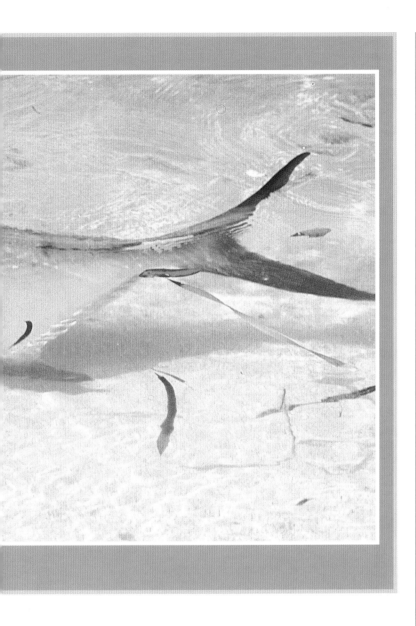

least glare occurs on the water. Sometimes it pays to plan your approach according to existing conditions. If there are white clouds in the sky, it is a good idea to move across the flats so that these clouds are not in the direction of movement. By approaching the clouds, the angler will be looking at the glare on the water, and even polarizing glasses will not penetrate the white reflection. Near islands or tall growth, the fish will be much easier to see if the angler looks in the direction where their dark green is reflected on the surface. This type of background allows the viewer to look clearly at the bottom.

Any unusual disturbance of the surface is also an indicator. If waves are moving in the opposite direction from the wind, something is pushing them. Often bonefish, especially, can be discovered by observing that some waves are moving in a different direction. And nervous waters (any small ripples) are a tip-off that something is creating the disturbance. Many kinds of fish, such as bonefish and sea trout, muddy the water as they root on the bottom. Try fishing where the mud is most dense or bright in colour. That is where the fish are active. By fishing a sinking fly through mud, you can often get terrific fishing. Once in Belize, we found a large mud, and caught bonefish for more than two hours on nearly every cast, using weighted bonefish flies. Casting into the muddiest area of the water, we allowed the fly to fall to the bottom. Then it was moved along in little hopping motions. Rarely did the fly travel more than a few yards before a bonefish found it.

Many fish can be caught near rays, such as stingrays and manarays. Rays often get their food by descending to the bottom, where they pound their heavy wings against it. This frightens shrimp, crabs and other food morsels from the grass and mud, which attempt to flee. The ray then grabs what it can. Rays are slow-moving, but predator species are much swifter and will often hover over the ray. If a shrimp or crab slips out from under the pounding wings, the predator often grabs it before the ray can. This means that the hovering predator is in a feeding mood. The ray creates a long streak of mud that is swept away by the current. By locating the muddiest water, and casting a fly a foot or so uptide from it, the fly can be retrieved over the ray, and into the mouth of a predator.

often miss seeing fish that are cruising below. To understand this, visualize someone looking at a person walking along a road. The viewer does not see the cattle in the field behind the walker. But if the viewer were looking at the cattle and the person·walked between him and the cattle, the walker would interrupt his vision and be seen. By looking at the bottom, any movement of fish between the bottom and the viewer is instantly noticed.

The angle of the sun is also important when looking for fish in the shallows. The best angle is to have the sun at your back, or at the back and a little to one side. That is when the

Planning your catch

Perhaps the main faccor in successfully hooking a saltwater fish, especially in the shallows, is how you approach and make your presentation. A noisy approach or a loud splash of the fly or line near the fish will frighten it. Because these predators are in the shallows and they know they can be seen easily, they are wary and will flee to the depths at the slightest indication of alarm. So the approach to such fish must be silent and carefully planned, and the presentation of the fly must be very correct.

When feeding, most predators working a flat approach it from the downtide side. Therefore, if the tide is flowing from the north to the south, the fish will enter the flat usually from the south, working into the current. The reason is that the tide carries the scent of their prey to them. It is amazing how far fish can smell shrimp, crabs and other food. In fact, some experienced anglers will anchor uptide on a white sand spot. They deposit chum (cut shrimp, conch crab or other fish food) in a sealed pipe drilled with holes to carry the scent to the fish but not allowing them to eat it, or scatter the bait on a white spot on the bottom. Smelling the bait more than 100 yards (91 m) down current, fish will come into the white sand. This makes them easier for the angler to see, so an accurate cast can be made.

It is good to understand that fish feed in the shallows much as a bird-dog hunts. The dog goes into a field downwind, lifts its nose and catches the scent of the birds as it manouvers through the field. Fish do the same thing. Entering a flat from the downtide side, a fish moves into the current, picking up the scent of shrimp crabs and other food. It wends itself back and forth into the current. Armed with this knowledge, an angler has an advantage. By wading or moving in a boat from the uptide side, the angler is in a good position to cast to approaching fish.

Presenting the fly correctly

Of paramount importance in both fresh and salt water is the awareness that, when a fly is offered to a fish, it expects to pursue this baitfish, crab, shrimp or other food source. It does not expect to be attacked by a prey species. Yet we often wrongly give that impression when we present a fly to a fish.

Any fly which is retrieved so that it approaches the fish from the rear, or is brought back directly at the fish, is an unnatural occurrence and the fish will usually not strike. The

very best method of retrieving to a fish is in the natural way. If the fish is swimming or facing into the tide, the angler should either wade or move the boat to one side and in front of the fish. Then a cast can be made upcurrent and a few feet to the far side ot the fish. As the fly is retrieved, the current draws it down to the fish. A few feet (1 m) in front of the fish, the fly makes a turn and begins to move upcurrent, back toward the angler. A fish is used to seeing prey species drift toward it on the current and then suddenly, realizing the danger, turn and move away. Such a retrieve is the best of all. Another good method: if a fish approaches you, throw the fly several feet (2-3 m) to one side and in front of the fish - not in a direct line with it. As the fly is brought back, the fish notices it appearing to escape.

Three incorrect or bad retrieves are often made. The angler casts well to the other side of the fish and begins to bring the fly back, but the current sweeps the fly downstream of the fish, and it comes from the side appearing to attack the fish. If a fish is swimming away from you, never throw over its back and retrieve it straight toward the fish. And perhaps the worst retrieve is to throw a fly to a fish lying directly below you, so that the fly lands behind the fish and approaches it from the rear - this almost always results in the fish fleeing.

A typical scene from the tropical and subtropical shallow flats, where fly-fishermen challenge permit and bonefish-among other species. The inset picture shows a tailing bonefish that stands on its nose digging out morsels of food with its tail protruding above the surface.

Flyfishing offshore

Flyfishing in water deeper than 10 feet (3 m), and on the open sea, requires different techniques than fishing in the shallows. In most cases something is used to lure the fish to the angler. Then a fly is presented. One common method is trolling a lure until a fish is hooked and brought near the boat. Many species tend to swim in schools, and others follow the hooked fish to the boat where the angler can make his presentation. Chuggers, sometimes called bloopers, are another way of luring fish within range of the fly caster. A large, floating casting plug devoid of hooks, with a scooped face, is thrown out on the surface. By giving hard jerks on the rod, the lure makes a loud gurgling sound, which many fish find attractive. As they rise to attack the plug, the fly is dropped nearby, usually resulting in a strike. Another method of luring fish is to chum. Ground or chopped pieces of fish, or sometimes even small whole fish, are sent overboard on the tide. Fish are lured to the food source, where the angler can make his cast. This is perhaps the most commonly used method of luring fish within casting range on open water.

Another method is used by billfishermen seeking marlin and sailfish. A hookless bait or artificial lure (called a teaser) is trolled on the ocean to attract a billfish. The angler has a partner who manipulates the teaser. The fish attacks the bait and mauls it, while the teaser is pulled closer. When the enraged fish is lured within a few feet of the boat, the teaser is jerked out of the water and the fly is placed in front of the billfish – which usually attacks it.

The use of lead-core shooting heads, and extremely fast-sinking fly lines that are loaded with lead dust, also allows anglers to fish to depths of 60 feet (20 m) if the tide is not running too strongly. This is often slow fishing, but anglers who are willing to cast the fast-sinking lines and allow them to descend into the depths are catching some very large reef species.

The flyfisherman waits for a fish to show over deep water. Sometimes one can lure the fish up to the surface and closer to the boat so as to cast at them more easily.

Poppers are used mainly in the USA when fishing for cobia, shark and sailfish. These bugs, having a flat or bowl-shaped front part, are often made of plastic, cork or balsa wood. But foam rubber material has become ever more common, since even big bugs are then easy and simple to cast. Popping bugs emit their sound when they scuttle across the surface as you take in the line fast. This sound may be fairly loud and probably makes the fish think some large prey is fleeing. It certainly seems attractive to many saltwater species and often triggers strikes.

Divers are bugs tied with deer hair. For fishing in shallow water, this Dahlberg Diver is superb, although bugs are usually heavy and hard to cast. Most typically, they have a deerhair head that is trimmed to slope backward in a conical shape. Like many other bugs, this one has a hook shield of monofilament nylon line, so as not to snag on underwater plants. It can be fished floating - by taking it in with jerks at the surface, to make a popping sound - and as a streamer, whose slithering movements seem very attractive to fish.

Sliders are a variant of popping bugs, with a conical front body. Due to its streamlined, rocket-like tip, the fly is easy to cast even in windy weather. It also moves more quietly and calmly in the water, which is most useful if you are after shy fish in the shallows. This type of fly is meant to imitate small, wounded prey fish at the surface - that is, rather easily caught ones. The colour of a slider has little importance, whereas its size and the way it is fished at the surface often determine whether or not the fish will attack it.

Saltwater flies

Size, colour, shape, and sink rate are all important factors when considering flies to catch saltwater fish. Size is perhaps the most important. Some fish, such as bonefish, have a small mouth; others, such as cobia, snappers and groupers all have large mouths. Offering a 5-in (13 cm) fly to a bonefish is almost certain to result in a refusal. And presenting a very small fly to a big fish with a large mouth will rarely convince the fish to strike. Bonito, for example, roam the world's seas, and they seem to prefer feeding on small 2-3 in (5-8 cm) slim minnows. A streamer fly that imitates these baits will do well. Cobia, sharks, and many other species all want larger flies. Cobia are a good example of where size is often vital to drawing a strike. Even a big 10-in (25 cm) bulky sailfish fly will often be refused by this fish. But a large popping bug that makes considerable noise will often result in a powerful strike. I believe that the popper, though smaller than a streamer, creates so much disturbance that it persuades cobia and other species that here is a much larger prey - and so they strike. Barracudas often scorn streamer flies, but a 0.5-1.0 (2-3 cm)

popping bug that is manipulated quickly across the surface will often cause them to hit. Apparently such a disturbance creates the impression that here is something large and edible that is rapidly getting away.

Frequently size is more important in fly patterns than how the fly is dressed. For some species, however, colour often plays a key role in whether the fish will strike. Striped bass and European bass often like a certain colour better than others. This can vary during the same day, so it pays to experiment with these fish. Sea trout and weakfish will often prefer a chartreuse or bright yellow colour. Fish that live on reefs, where the fly is fished at least 10-30 ft (3-9 m) down, can often be caught sooner on flies that have the dressing made from fluorescent colours, which can be seen in their true tints at greater depths. Snook seem to go for bright yellow combinations. Many offshore species are best caught on streamer flies that have a blue or green back and white belly. Almost all streamer flies fished in open waters are better if their belly is white, the colour of every prey species that predators feed upon.

Surface flies

The most popular surface flies are popping bugs. They were made originally of cork, then of balsa wood, but lately the use of closed-cell foam plastics has increased. These are much lighter and easier to cast, and fairly large bugs can be made that weigh far less than those of the same size in cork or balsa wood. The buoys used by commercial fishermen to mark their traps and pots are an excellent material to fashion popping bugs from. Tough, very light and easy to work with, they make superb popping bugs.

Poppers come in two different designs. The standard bug is one with a flat or cup-forward face. On the retrieve, the line is stripped quickly and the bug moves forward, pushing water and making a popping sound. This is very attractive to many species of saltwater fish. The other type of popping bug is called a slider, shaped more like the cone on a rocket or the front end of a bullet. This pointed bug makes little disturbance on the surface. In situations where fish are wary, or easily alarmed

when in shallow water, the slider can be manipulated without a great deal of disturbance, which may frighten the fish. The slider is usually tied to resemble a minnow or baitfish. It represents an injured minnow, struggling on the surface - appearing to be an easy meal for a predator. Many experienced anglers, myself included, feel that the colour of a popping bug is not important. What is important is the size of the bug and how it is manipulated on the surface.

Deer-hair popping bugs are rarely used in salt water, but are a favourite of many freshwater fishermen. The deer-hair bug is bulky, difficult to cast against the ever-present sea breeze; and after being fished for a while, the deer hair soaks up water. This makes it heavier and more difficult to cast, and it doesn't work as well on the surface. However, one deer bug is superb in shallow saltwater situations around the world: the Dahlberg Diver. This has a body and wing of a baitfish, but the head is made from spun deer hair and clipped. The result is a cone-shaped head that slants

back to a large collar. When manipulated on the surface, the bug makes a popping sound. Yet if the retrieve is constant, the bug dives under the water and swims in a wobbling motion. Thus, the lure can be worked as a popper, streamer, or sometimes a combination of the two. It can be popped several times, then made to dive and swim a short distance. The retrieve is stopped and the bug slowly rises to the surface, where the retrieve can be repeated over and over. The bug is almost always dressed with a monofilament weed guard, which allows it to be cast into or near brush, without fear of getting it snagged in the trees.

Below: Coastal flyfishing along the shallow coasts of northern Europe is sometimes extraordinarily rewarding. Common catches are garfish (see inset), sea trout, mackerel, cod and coalfish.

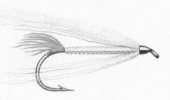

This streamer, of the synthetic material organza, is very common for coastal flyfishing in southern Scandinavia. An organza streamer nicely imitates a little silvery prey fish, and is thus extremely effective in catching, for example, sea trout. Like most streamers, this one is usually tied on straight-eyed hooks 3-5 cm (1.2-2.0 in) long

Ullsocken is a Swedish fly that has long been used in the country's southern salmon and sea-trout rivers. But coastal flyfishermen discovered that it can also be fished as an imitation of a ragworm. Not least the sea trout, which seek shallow coves during the spring in order to feast on these hairy worms, find it hard to resist the fly. Its tail is tied with red wool, the body of peacock herl or floss, and the hackle of brown cock or hen hackle feather.

The above streamer has been given a wing of marabou feathers, and represents an effective type for several species. It can naturally also be tied with hair wings, but its movement in the water is then less lively. The fly can be fished either superficially or deep for sea trout, garfish, mackerel, cod, coalfish and many other species. The wing colours may be varied, yet green, red, yellow, orange and/or blue flies have proved good.

Fly patterns
Tying a wet fly Fiery Brown

1. Fastening the tail:

Attach the tying thread and cut a V shape of the tail material (for any fly with a tail of hackle feathers). Wind the feather tight with some turns of the thread (Photo 1). Straighten up the feather and pull it toward the hook eye. Clip off the feather stem.

2. Attaching tinsel

(also floss silk, wool yarn, copper wire etc.): Make an eye of the tinsel around the tying thread (Photo 2). Draw the thread up to breast height and let the tinsel eye slide in toward the hook. Then wind the thread until about 2 mm behind the hook eye (Photo 3).

3. Tying in the body:

Go back with the tying thread to the hook bend, and stop about 2 mm from the tail. Spin the dubbing material around the thread and wind the thread in even turns, first backward and then forth toward the hook eye. Wind the tinsel in even turns until 2-3 mm behind the hook eye (Photo 4).

4. Tying in the hackle:

Cut a V in the hackle feather and stroke the fibres backward, so that only four fibres remain on each side of the stem. Fasten the feather with some turns of the tying thread (Photo 5). Pull the feather in toward the head and clip off. Repeat this process four times, but now place the feather twice somewhat to the right and twice to the left. The fly's hackle is now complete (Photo 6).

5. Tying in the wing:

Clip the wing from two mallard feathers and lay them against each other – front side against back side. Place the feathers directly over the fly body. Form an eye with the tying thread and pull straight upward. Repeat this twice so that the wing is well attached (Photo 7). Cut off excess wing material as near the thread as possible.

6. Tying the head:

Change to black tying thread and wind it tight at the hook eye. Then wind back toward the wing so that the white thread is fastened. Clip off the white thread and form the head with the black thread. Make a whip-finish knot, clip off the black thread, and coat the head with clear varnish (Photo 8). The fly is complete.

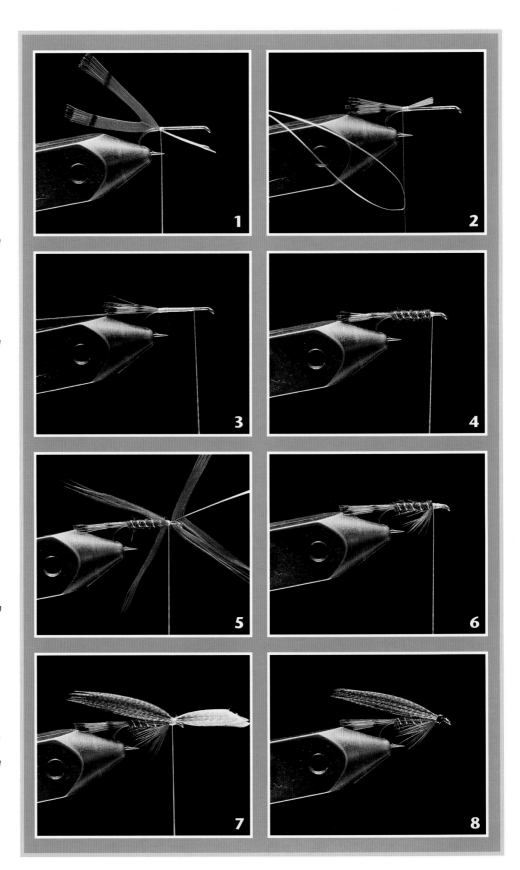

Tying a dry fly
Black Gnat variant

1. Tie in the tail and body:

Fasten the tying thread and tie the tail in the same way as on the wet fly, but repeat twice to give the dry fly better buoyancy. Wind the thread toward the hook eye in even turns. Go back with the thread toward the hook bend, stopping about 2 mm from the tail. Attach the dubbing and wind first backward, then forward so that 2/3 of the hook shaft is covered with dubbing, and possibly trim it (Photo 1).

2. Tie in the wing:

Mix black and natural deer hairs (in equal proportions). Hold the bunch of hair between your thumb and middle finger over the hook – with the hair tips forward – and fasten it with three turns of tying thread. Wind some more turns, and clip off the hairs just in front of the body (Photo 2).

3. Tie in the hackle:

To make a durable hackle, first lay a piece of black tying thread in an eye around the white thread and fasten it. Then lay the hackle over the black thread and fasten with the white thread (Photo 3). Wind the thread about 15 turns forward to the wing and past it, so that it rises (Photo 4). Clip off the hackle stem and the black thread as close as possible to the white thread (Photo 5).

Dub thinly with black dubbing around the black thread. Hold the thread and the hackle together and pinch them tightly with hackle pliers. Twist about 15 turns, and wrap tightly around the hook by going forward and laying each turn just in front of the last. Wind 5-6 turns and fasten with some turns of white thread. Stroke the wing and hackle backward with your fingers and attach securely with the thread (Photo 6).

4. Tie the head (black):

Use black tying thread and wind it in the same way as on the wet fly. Conclude with a whip-finish knot and varnish the head. The dry fly is complete (Photo 7).

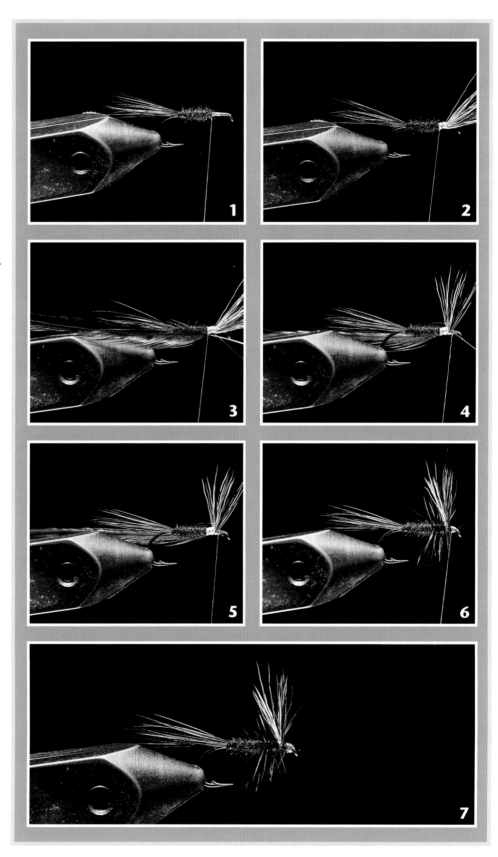

Tying a shrimp fly

Ally's Shrimp

1. Tie in the tail and body:

Wind on the white tying thread and attach the tinsel in the same way as previously. Tie in the tail – as long as the hook – and wind the thread forward to half the body. Clip off the hairs where the head will later begin (Photo 1).

2. Tie in floss and ribbing:

Attach the red floss silk with the tying thread. Wind the silk first backward, then forward, and attach to the body middle. Wind the thread up to the head, attach the black floss, wind backward and then forward, and fasten the floss. Rib with five turns of tinsel (Photo 2).

3. Tie in the wing:

First attach the overwing, then the underwing. Varnish at the fastening to make the wing more durable (Photo 3). Next, choose a centre-tip feather of golden pheasant, ensuring that the feather is as long as the hook. Clip off a bit of the stem, run it into the hook eye, and lay the feather directly over the hook. Hold it between your thumb and middle finger, and wind four loose turns with the tying thread. Hold the hackle stem and pull the feather forward until the squirrel hairs' white tops are visible. Wind two loose turns of thread and pull upward to fasten the feather (Photo 4). Holding the feather between your thumb and middle finger, clip off the stem – first in front of the hook eye, then behind.

4. Tie in the hackle:

Cut a V in one of the hackle feathers. Stroke backward so that only four fibres remain on each side of the stem, and wind it on with a loose turn of tying thread (Photo 5). Clip off the hackle and pull the thread tight. Repeat this process about ten times, but place the feathers somewhat to the right and left, so that the hackle forms a collar round the body.

5. Tie the stripe and head:

Fasten the floss silk with two turns of the tying thread, just before the hackle collar. Wind three turns of floss toward the hook eye to tie the stripe. Attach the floss with one turn of thread, and hold it at about a 45-degree angle to the hook bend (this prevents the floss fibres from sticking up). Repeat and fasten with two turns of thread. Change to red thread and wind it from the front back toward the stripe. Add 1-2 turns around the white thread, clip it off, and form the head with the red thread. Make a whip-finish knot, clip off the tying thread, and varnish the head (Photo 6). The fly is complete.

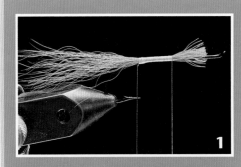
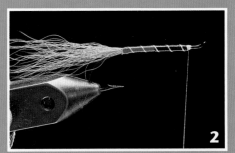

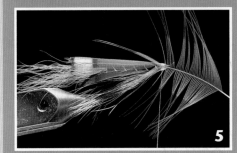

Five tips that simplify flytying:

Use white tying thread.

Thus, when you use light materials in the body or tag, they will be kept even when the fly is in the water. But if black tying thread is used, the fly instead becomes grayish, since the thread then shines through the material.

Use fine cotton gloves when you tie in floss silk.

The floss silk will then not break during the tying, and light colors will keep the same tone throughout the body (hands are almost always a bit dirty, especially after a couple of hours of tying, which often colours the silk).

Thin the flytying varnish with pure acetone in equal proportions.

The varnish then penetrates the thread better, making the fly more durable.

Clip off the material just in front of the head.

This gives an even body, which is very important, particularly when you are to tie a body of flat gold or silver tinsel.

Use your thumb and middle finger when tying wings.

The wing will thus sit quite straight. Using your thumb and forefinger increases the risk of tying the wing in crooked.

Tying a salmon fly
IQ Black Dawn

1. Tie a tag: Attach the tinsel with the tying thread as shown previously. Wind the tinsel with tight, even turns toward the hook bend; stop just over the barb, and wind the thread back to the hook tip. Then wind the tinsel toward the hook tip. Be careful that the turns lie densely and do not overlap each other. Fasten the tinsel with some thread turns and clip it off about 3 mm behind the hook eye. Wind the thread in tight turns to 3 mm behind the hook eye, make a whip-finish knot, and clip off the thread. Varnish the tag 3-4 times for greater durability, letting the tag dry well after each time.

2. Tie in the tail: Cut a V in one of the hackle feathers and stroke the fibres backward, so that three fibres remain on each side of every stem. Tie in the hackle with two turns of thread, just where the fibres divide, and pull the hackle toward the hook eye until the tail is 1 1/2 times as high as the hook gap. Fasten with two turns of thread. Clip off excess material near the thread. Repeat three times.

3. Tie in the butt: Attach floss silk with a turn of tying thread on the hook's underside (see Ally's Shrimp, point 5), as close as possible to the clipped hackle. Wind the floss three turns back toward the hook bend, then three turns forward. Holding the floss stretched downward, run the thread behind and around it. Fasten it with a turn of thread while pulling the floss forward. Wind some more turns, and clip off the floss about 3 mm behind the hook eye. Varnish the butt twice (see Photo 1).

4. Tie in the body and the body hackle: Attach the rib floss and body tinsel to the hook shaft's underside, as near the butt as possible. Wind the thread in tight, even turns forward and stop at the body middle. Clip off the floss and

tinsel 2-3 mm behind the hook eye. Fasten the mylar tinsel to the hook shaft's underside, with the gold side toward the shaft. Wind the tinsel backward in tight turns that do not overlap. At the butt, the tinsel is wound forward and fastened with thread. Clip off excess tinsel 2-3 mm behind the hook eye (Photo 2). Take a black cock hackle with fibres as long as the hook gap's height, wet your fingers and stroke the fibres backward. Tie in the hackle feather where the fibres parted, on the hook shaft's underside at the end of the tinsel body. Dub crystal seal on the thread and wind the body up toward the head. Rib the body with five even turns of the tinsel and fasten with the thread. Wind the floss just behind the tinsel and fasten. Then wind the body hackle forward so that each turn lies exactly behind the floss, and finish with two turns in front of the dubbing. Secure with the thread and clip off excess material (Photo 3).

5. Tie in the hackle and wing: Attach the hackle so that the fibres end just behind the hook bend (see Fiery Brown, point 4). Clip off the excess and varnish the fibre ends.
Take two orange hackle feathers, from the nape's left and right sides; lay them together so that the tips lie level. Remove the fluff where they will be wound on. Clip off the stems, but leave 2 mm and tie the feathers with some loose turns of thread. Wind three more turns and fasten by pulling the thread straight up; varnish the winding (Photo 4). Tie in two red flashabou – as long as the hackle feathers – on each side. Trim and varnish. Attach the fox hairs with some turns of thread, clip off the excess, and varnish.

6. Tie in a stripe (see also Ally's Shrimp, point 5): Attach the floss on the hook shaft's underside just in front of the hackle, and wind three turns. Secure with some turns of tying thread. Change to black thread, wind toward the stripe, and form the head as described previously. Conclude with a whip-finish knot and varnish the head 3-4 times with diluted varnish. The salmon fly is complete (Photo 5).

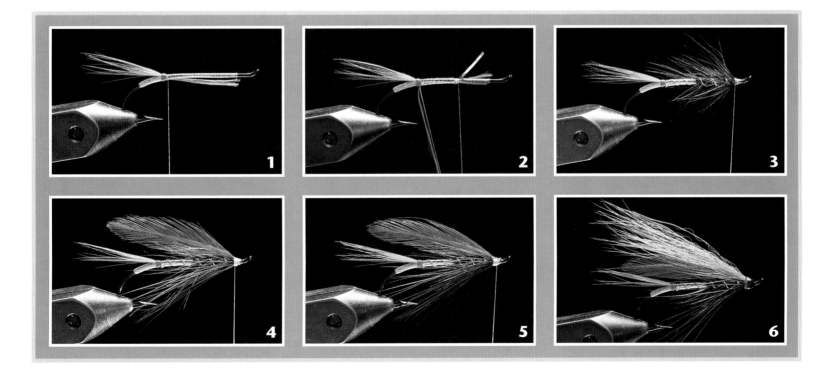

Dry flies

Greenwell's Glory (deer-hair variant)
Tying thread: yellow, waxed 8/0
Body: yellow waxed tying thread
Ribbing: fine oval gold tinsel
Wing: brown and natural deer hair, half of each
Hackle: light furnace cock hackle
Head: yellow tying thread

This classic fly pattern is to imitate yellow-green mayflies, and is fished mainly in trout waters.

Royal Wulff
Tying thread: white 8/0
Tail: white deer hair (or natural deer hair)
Body: peacock herl, back and front, with red floss silk between
Wing: white deer hair (or natural deer hair)
Hackle: two brown cock hackles
Head: black tying thread, possibly with a stripe of fluorescent orange floss silk

This attractor fly is gladly taken by salmon, trout, char, grayling and steelhead in both still and flowing waters.

Coch-Y-Bondhu
Tying thread: white 8/0
Tag: fine oval gold tinsel
Body: peacock herl
Hackle: brown cock hackle
Head: black or white tying thread

This all-round pattern fishes well for trout, grayling and char.

Quill Gordon (deer-hair variant)
Tying thread: white 8/0
Tail: brown deer hair
Body: peeled stem from peacock herl
Wing: brown deer hair
Hackle: dark blue dun cock hackle
Head: black or white tying thread

This fly imitates brown mayflies and is chiefly used for trout, but char and grayling are also fond of it.

Dry flies

Black Gnat
Tying thread: black or white 8/0
Tail: black cock hackle
Body: black crystal seal or crystal hare's ear-dubbing
Wing: black and brown deer hair, half of each
Hackle: black cock, twisted with same material as the body
Head: black or white tying thread

Adams (deer-hair variant)
Tying thread: white 8/0
Tail: grizzly and brown cock
Body: gray dubbing
Wing: brown deer hair
Hackle: grizzly and brown cock hackle
Head: black tying thread

Harkrank (Daddy LongLegs)
Tying thread: white 8/0
Body: natural deer hair
Legs: tail feather from golden pheasant, with knee and ankle joints
Wing: brown-coloured grizzly cock hackle
Hackle: grizzly cock saddle hackle
Head: white tying thread

Elk Hair Caddis (deer-hair variant)
Tying thread: white 8/0 • Body: green dubbing
Body hackle: brown cock saddle hackle, twisted with same material as the body
Wing: natural-coloured deer hair
Head: white tying thread

This pattern can be made in different colour variants and sizes to imitate local caddis flies.

Bäckslända (stonefly)
Tying thread: white 8/0
Tail: teal from mallard
Body: yellow dubbing
Body hackle: brown cock saddle hackle, twisted with same material as the body
Wing: black jumbo nape
Thorax: brown cock saddle hackle, twisted with same material as the body
Antennae: teal from mallard
Head: white tying thread

Sedge Variant
Tying thread: white 8/0
Tail: brown deer hair
Body: hare's ear
Wing: nape feather from ring-necked pheasant
Thorax: brown cock, twisted with body material
Head: white tying thread

The pattern can be made in different colour variants and sizes to imitate mayflies.

Nymphs and Flymphs

Hare's Ear Larva (weighted)
Tying thread: white 8/0
Body: light hare's ear
Body hackle: brown cock saddle hackle,
  twisted with same material as the body
Thorax: Weight with copper wire and dub with
  dark hare's ear; pick out some hairs to imitate legs
Head: white or black tying thread

Deep Sparkle Pupa
Tying thread: white 8/0
Rear body: green dubbing and yellow antron yarn
Hackle: brown hen hackle
Front body: dark hare's ear
Head: brown tying thread

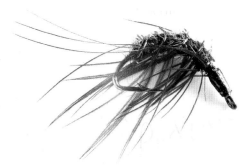

Gammarus
Tying thread: brown 8/0
Body: dark hare's ear
Ribbing: oval silver tinsel
Hackle: brown hen hackle
Carapace: pearl flashabou
Head: brown tying thread

*A light variant of Gammarus is obtained by using light
hare's ear and light brown hen hackle. In the same way
green Gammarus imitations are made.*

Hare's Ear Flymph
Tying thread: white 8/0
Tail: brown partridge
Body: dark hare's ear
Hackle: light blue dun hen hackle,
  twisted with same material as the body
Head: white tying thread

*For light variants, the light part
of the hare's ear is used.*

Nymphs and Flymphs

Yellow Flymph
Tying thread: white 8/0
Tail: brown partridge
Body: yellow dubbing
Hackle: light brown hen hackle,
 twisted with light hare's ear
Head: white tying thread

Green Damselfly Nymph
Tying thread: white 8/0
Tail: green marabou
Body: green marabou
Ribbing: green copper wire
Thorax: green pearl mylar
Eyes: peacock herl
Head: black 8/0

MayFly Flymph
Tying thread: white 8/0
Tail: brown partridge
Body: hare's ear
Ribbing: white tying thread
Hackle: brown partridge
Head: white tying thread

Free-living Green Caddis Fly Larva
Tying thread: white 8/0
Body: clear green dubbing
Hackle: brown hen hackle,
 twisted with same material as the body
Head: black tying thread

Black Martinez (mylar variant)
Tying thread: black 8/0
Tail: natural guinea hen
Body: black dubbing
Ribbing: copper wire
Thorax: green pearl mylar
Hackle: grizzly hen

Wet flies

Fiery Brown
Tying thread: white 8/0
Tail: orange-coloured tippets from golden pheasant
Body: fiery brown-coloured dubbing
Ribbing: oval silver tinsel
Hackle: orange to fiery brown-coloured cock
Wing: mallard
Head: black tying thread

Black Zulu
Tying thread: black or white 8/0
Tail: red wool yarn
Body: black dubbing
Ribbing: oval silver tinsel
Hackle: black hen hackle
Head: black tying thread

Coachman
Tying thread: white 8/0
Tag: fine oval gold tinsel
Body: peacock herl
Wing: white duck or substitute
Hackle: brown cock hackle
Head: black tying thread

Red Tag
Tying thread: white 8/0
Tail: red wool yarn
Body: peacock herl
Hackle: brown cock hackle
Head: black tying thread

Teal and Silver
Tying thread: white 8/0
Body: flat silver tinsel
Ribbing: oval silver tinsel
Wing: teal feather from mallard
Hackle: blue cock hackle
Head: black tying thread

Streamers

Black Nosed Dose (mylar variant)
Tying thread: white 8/0
Tail: red wool yarn
Body: holographic silver mylar, with
a band of red tying thread
Wing: white, black and brown hair
with some strands of peacock angel hair
between the black and brown
Head: black tying thread

Black and Gold (mylar variant)
Tying thread: white 8/0
Body: holographic gold mylar, witha band of
white tying thread
Wing: black hair mixed with a little peacock angel hair
Head: black tying thread

Teal and Blue (hairwing)
Tying thread: black or white 8/0 • *Tail:* yellow cock hackle
Body: flat silver tinsel • *Ribbing:* oval silver tinsel
Wing: white squirrel • *Hackle:* peacock-blue cock hackle
Head: black tying thread

Black Satan
Tying thread: white or black 8/0
Tail: red cock hackle
Body: black dubbing or floss
Ribbing: oval silver tinsel
Wing: black hair mixed with a
few strands of red angel hair
Hackle: black cock hackle
Head: black tying thread

IQ Sculpin
Tying thread: white 8/0
Tail: four brown-coloured grizzly hackle
Body: brown ice chenille
Body hackle: brown-coloured grizzly hackle twisted with ice chenille
Eyes: yellow-black doll eyes • *Head:* small, of white tying thread

*This fly can be tied in several combinations of
colours by replacing the hackle and chenille.*

Sea-trout flies

Ally's Shrimp
Tying thread: *white 8/0*
Tail: *orange bucktail with 2-4 pearl*
flashabou or crystal flash
Body: *black and red floss, half of each*
Ribbing: *oval gold tinsel*
Wing: *over- and underwing of white squirrel, with tippet*
feather from golden pheasant on top
Hackle: *orange cock*
Head: *red tying thread, possibly with a stripe of*
fluorescent orange floss

Hare's Ear Shrimp
Tying thread: *white 8/0*
Tail: *light hair from hare's mask*
Eyes: *0.50-mm nylon*
Body: *light hare's ear*
Back: *10-15 pearl flashabou, varnished*
Head: *white tying thread*

This fly is mainly used for coastal sea-trout fishing.

Ragworm / Leech imitation
Tying thread: *white 8/0*
Rear hook: *Hackle: orange marabou*
Head: *red tying thread, possibly with a stripe of*
fluorescent orange floss
Body: *black ice chenille, braided with dycroon 0.22 mm*
Front hook: *Body: black ice chenille*
Head: *white or red tying thread, possibly with a stripe of*
fluorescent orange floss

*This fly is superb when fishing both in lakes and along
the coast, but is also widely thought to fish well for trout,
char, pike and bass.*

March Brown Silver
Tying thread: *white 8/0*
Tail: *brown partridge*
Body: *flat silver tinsel*
Ribbing: *oval silver tinsel*
Wing: *pheasant hen or substitute*
Hackle: *brown partridge*
Head: *black tying thread, possibly with a stripe of*
light-brown floss

This classic fly is also excellent for salmon.

IQ Shrimp
Tying thread: *white 8/0*
Tail: *brown-orange fox with copper angel hair*
Body: *brown-orange crystal seal*
Ribbing: *oval gold tinsel*
Wing: *over- and underwing of brown-orange fox.*
Above the wing an orange-coloured tippet from golden
pheasant is tied in as a back.
Hackle: *brown-orange cock*
Head: *red tying thread, possibly with a stripe of*
fluorescent orange floss

Salmon flies

Blue Charm (hairwing variant)

Tying thread: white 8/0 • *Tag:* oval gold tinsel with yellow floss
Tail: yellow cock hackle • *Butt:* black ostrich
Body: dubbed with black crystal seal
Ribbing: oval silver tinsel • *Hackle:* blue cock
Wing: (1) two blue cock feathers, back to back; (2) two to four pearl
  flashabou, one or two on each side of the hackle; (3) brown fox
Head: black tying thread, possibly with a stripe of light-blue floss

Bomber

Tying thread: white 6/0
Tail: white squirrel • *Body:* natural deer hair
Body hackle: Palmer-wound grizzly hackle
Antennae: white squirrel • *Head:* white or black tying thread

*Bomber can be made in many colour variants and sizes.
The fly is an excellent attractor for both salmon and sea trout,
but also works well for other species such as steelhead and pike.*

Sunray Shadow

Tying thread: white 6/0
Body: plastic tube • *Wing:* white squirrel with black goat or fox over.
  Peacock angel hair mixed over the wing.
Head: black tying thread, possibly with a stripe of fluorescent
  orange floss

This fly is also fine for sea-trout fishing in flowing waters.

IQ Black Dawn

Tying thread: white 8/0 • *Tag:* oval gold tinsel, varnished
Tail: three deep-orange hackle • *Butt:* fluorescent orange floss
Body: rear half of flat gold tinsel, front half of black and gold
  crystal seal
Ribbing: oval gold tinsel and fluorescent orange floss
Body hackle: black hackle, but only over the front half
Hackle: black heron or long, soft cock hackle until just behind
  the hook bend
Wing: (1) deep-orange hackle pair, back to back; (2) two red
  flashabou on each side of the hackle; (3) gold-brown fox,
  or raccoon body hair
Head: black tying thread, possibly with a stripe of fluorescent
  orange floss

Green Highlander (hairwing variant)

Tying thread: white 8/0
Tag: oval silver tinsel and yellow floss • *Tail:* yellow cock hackle
Butt: black ostrich herl
Body: 1/3 yellow floss, 2/3 green dubbing
Ribbing: oval silver tinsel • *Body hackle:* green cock hackle
Hackle: yellow cock hackle
Wing: (1) two green cock hackle, tied back to back; (2) two pearl
  flashabou, one on each side of the hackle; (3) yellow, orange
  and brown fox hair, in equal parts, with a strip of
  golden-brown fox hair on top
Head: black tying thread, possibly with a stripe of fluorescent
  green floss

This classic salmon fly fishes best in clear water and sunshine.

Pike flies

Red Popper (deer hair)
Tying thread: red 6/0
Tail: four red and four grizzly hackle, with around ten red holographic flashabou
Hackle: red and grizzly cock hackle
Body: red deer hair; can also be made of balsa wood
Eyes: yellow-black doll eyes

This fly can be made in many colour variants.

Slider (deer hair)
Tying thread: white 6/0
Tail: four orange-coloured grizzly cock hackle and four grizzly cock hackle, with around ten yellow holographic flashabou
Hackle: grizzly and orange-coloured grizzly
Body: white deer hair as belly, and orange deer hair with strips of black deer hair
Eyes: yellow-black doll eyes

This fly can also be tied in green, red, blue or other variants by replacing all the orange with such a colour.

Bullet Frog
Tying thread: white 6/0 • *Body:* yellow and green deer tail
Leg: yellow and green deer tail • *Eyes:* yellow-black doll eyes

Soft Hackle Fly
Tying thread: white 6/0
Wing: twisted yellow, green and blue marabou
Hackle: teal from mallard
Head: white tying thread, possibly with a stripe of light-blue floss

This fly can also be tied in countless colour variants.

Tarpon Streamer
Tying thread: white or red 6/0
Tail: four white and grizzly cock hackle, with around ten silver holographic flashabou
Hackle: blue cock hackle
Cheeks: around ten silver holographic flashabou on each side
Eyes: silver chain
Body: red tying thread, varnished

This fly can be tied in countless colour variants.

Salt-water flies

Cockroach
Tying thread: black 6/0
Tail: four grizzly hackle
Hackle: brown deer hair
Head: black tying thread, possibly with a stripe
   of light-brown floss

Lefty's Deceiver
Tying thread: white 6/0
Tail: four white cock hackle, with two holographic flashabou fibres
Hackle: blue deer tail
Head: white tying thread, possibly with a stripe of light-blue floss

This fly occurs in many colour variants.

Strawberry Blonde
Tying thread: white 6/0
Tail: orange hair with orange angel hair
Body: flat silver tinsel
Wing: red hair with red angel hair
Head: white tying thread, possibly with a stripe of red floss

The Blonde series exists in several colour variants; see page 218.

Sea Ducer
Tying thread: white 6/0
Tail: six yellow cock hackle, two grizzly hackle, and
   around ten silver holographic flashabou strands
Body: two or three yellow cock hackle
Hackle: two red cock hackle
Head: black tying thread, possibly with a stripe of
   fluorescent orange floss

Hagen Sand's Bonefish Bucktail (variant)
Tying thread: white 6/0
Wing: four yellow cock hackle and four grizzly hackle, tied in back
   to back as two pairs over each other
Hackle: white deer tail
Head: ice chenille with yellow-black doll eyes

The original has a black head of tying thread with painted eyes
in yellow and black.

Index